How to Build Your Own Working 16-Bit Microcomputer

Other TAB books by the author:

No. 771 *Integrated Circuits Guidebook*
No. 861 *Display Electronics*
No. 960 *IC Function Locator*
No. 1000 *57 Practical Programs & Games in BASIC*
No. 1055 *The BASIC Cookbook*
No. 1085 *24 Tested, Ready-to-Run Game Programs in BASIC*
No. 1095 *Programs in BASIC for Electronic Engineers, Technicians & Experimenters*

How to Build Your Own Working 16-Bit Microcomputer

By Ken Tracton

TAB BOOKS
BLUE RIDGE SUMMIT, PA. 17214

FIRST EDITION

FIRST PRINTING—APRIL 1979
SECOND PRINTING—MAY 1980

Printed in the United States of America

Library of Congress Cataloging in Publication Data

Tracton, Ken.
How to build your own working 16-bit microcomputer.

Includes index.
1. Microcomputers—Design and construction—Amateurs' manuals. I. Title.
TK9969.T7 621.3819'5 78-10353
ISBN 0-8306-9813-2 pbk.

Cover photo courtesy of Electronic Technician/Dealer magazine.

Preface

Microprocessors, those tiny slices of processing power, are rapidly growing more potent. The first microprocessor was suitable only for simple controller operations (such as the control unit of a microwave oven). Its immediate successors had a greatly increased instruction set, but were limited to 4-bit data chunks. These chips remain with us, as the processors in calculators. Within a year, both 8- and 12-bit units reached the market, and the microcomputer as we know it was born. Now, we are able to build 16-bit processors that can compete on equal terms with mini computers, both in speed and in capability.

One such device, the 9900 CPU by Texas Instruments, is widely considered to be the most advanced single-chip processor yet built. This text describes how to design a working *micro-computer* with the 9900 and its support family.

It begins with a minimum unit, useful for machine language and control functions, and progresses to an information processing system that can include time-sharing, a variety of languages, floppy-discs, disc-drives, cassette tape units, and a host of different terminals. En route, it discusses each type of interface required, how to use it, and how, on occasion, to circumvent its necessity.

The appendices include 9900 instruction codes, pinouts of the 9900 support chips as described in the text, and a listing of the ASCII code in near-universal use.

I would like to thank Mr. Alec Grynspan, who compiled the vast amount of data required for this text and assisted me in many different capacities. I must also give special thanks to Mr. Dave Campbell, representative of Texas Instruments for his cheerful and understanding help which made this book possible, and of course Texas Instruments who created the 9900 family of micro-processor devices and peripherals, who graciously supplied the materials that allowed me to evaluate the information.

Ken Tracton

Contents

1 Introduction to Microprocessors

The first microprocessors were 4-bit types which handled data as 4-bit nybbles. The earliest of this new breed of machines, the Intel 4004, was a major breakthrough. It was quickly followed by the Intel 4040, and the National Semiconductor IMP-4.

The 4-bit microprocessors are, for the most part, considered obsolete. The exceptions are the one-chip microcomputers, with storage and interfaces, as well as control on a single chip. These are excellent controllers and have been used in such devices as sewing machines, CRT controllers, and TV games.

An example is the TMS1000-series microprocessor, made by Texas Instruments (TI), consisting of the TMS1000, TMS1100, TMS1200, and TMS1300 processors. These consist of one-chip microprocessors containing from 1024 to 2048 bytes of read only memory (ROM), a central processing unit (CPU), 32 to 64 bytes (addressed as 64 to 128 nybbles) of random access memory (RAM) for a scratch pad, and simple input/output (I/O) logic.

These chips are incredibly low in cost when one considers their power and versatility; with their various kin, they have completely changed the electronics and controller fields.

Although the Intel 4004 set the world on its ear, the first 8-bit units, of which the Intel 8008 is the most famous, turned it upside down.

The smallest minicomputer being taken seriously were 8-bit (1 byte) processors, and suddenly there was a complete computer on a chip.

In actuality these first 8-bit machines were bigger versions of the 4-bit types and meant to be used as controllers, not as computers. Their instruction set and interfacing requirements were oriented towards process control. Even so, the hobbyists started using them for other purposes and quickly started up that class of systems called microcomputers.

Microcomputers are now used in such sophisticated devices as (a) pocket computers, more powerful than the early monsters in the computer industry; (b) desk-top computers, capable of serving such diverse users as car dealers and small motels and hotels; (c) office computers, for the accountant and business man; (d) TV games, of such sophistication that one of these units can play hundreds of different games, controlled by the insertion of a small tape cartridge, and (e) robots, capable of such far-ranging feats as controlling Mars and Jupiter probes to as mundane feats as delivering the office mail.

The number of 8-bit machines has grown enormously, and is always in flux, with newer models available almost daily. The following is a list of some of the better known 8-bit microprocessors:

- F8 by Fairchild
- 3870 by Mostek
- SC/MP by National Semiconductor
- 8080 family by Intel
- Z80 by Zilog
- 6800 family by Motorola
- 6500 family by MOS Technology
- 2650 family by Signetics
- COSMAC 1802 family by RCA

THE 12-BIT MICROPROCESSOR

This microprocessor is a lonely creature, standing by itself in terms of the number of variations available. The IM-6100 from Intersil duplicates the Digital Equipment Corp. (DEC) PDP-8 almost perfectly.

The PDP-8 has one enormous feature going for it that makes the soft-ware-compatible IM-6100 very popular and tempting, that is, the software of the PDP-8. It is this colossal amount of material that almost compensates for the primitive instruction set capability of the IM-6100.

In languages alone it outstrips any other microprocessor (as well as some much larger machines), having;

A) DIBOL	DEC business language
B) ALGOL-60	the subroutine definition language
C) FORTRAN	the most famous scientific language
D) SNOBOL	string manipulation language
E) APL	the mathematical language
F) LISP	the artificial intelligence language
G) BASIC	the most popular language of all
H) FOCAL	a supercalculator language
I) LIBRA	time-sharing FOCAL
J) MACRO	a macro-assembler for machine language users
K) LINK-EDITOR	for hooking everything together
L) DOS	for developing systems
M) TSS	time-sharing system

If the PDP-8 or IM6100 has all this power, then why, you may ask, isn't this book written solely on the construction of this machine? The main reason is that I feel that the TI TMS9900 microprocessor is fresh ground for the microcomputer user, with even more potential than the PDP-8.

Other reasons include the most advanced architecture of any true microprocessor is currently within the TMS9900; the TMS9900 has the greatest flexibility of any microprocessor yet developed; the TMS9900 has the best instruction set of any microprocessor, exceeding many minicomputers; and the software development pace for the TMS9900 is increasing exponentially.

While there are so-called microprocessors with power just as great as the TMS9900 (the DEC LSI-11 includes floating point as an option) they are either not as cost-effective or not as flexible (e.g., the LSI-11 could never be used as economically to control a CRT or other smart devices). The LSI-11/2 now consists of separate CPU, memory, and interface cards, but the CPU is not available as a chip or chip group without the card.

THE 16-BIT MACHINES

Just as the 8-bit microprocessors absorbed and expanded the low end of the minicomputer industry, the 16-bit versions are beginning to make themselves felt in the main stomping grounds of the minicomputer field.

The 16-bit unit, unlike its cousin the 8-bit type, is not really a microprocessor, but is in reality a minicomputer using large-scale integration (LSI) technology. The main 16-bit machines are;

- 9440 by Fairchild
- MicroNOVA by Data General
- CP1600 by General Instruments
- Pace by National Semiconductor
- TMS9900 family by Texas Instruments
- MC2 by Hewlett-Packard
- LSI-11 by DEC

The Fairchild 9440 is an exact duplicate, in terms of instruction set, of the Data General NOVA, while the Data General microNOVA is an extended version of the same machine, with built-in stack and hardware multiply and divide.

The DEC LSI-11 is an LSI version of their PDP-11 minicomputers.

The NOVA was designed as a 16-bit version of the 12-bit PDP-8 with added capabilities that eliminated some of the limitations inherent in the PDP-8. This does not mean that the instructions were simply expanded, but that the concept was expanded.

From this we can see that the IM6100, the 9440, the microNOVA, and the LSI-11 are all minicomputers in the guise of microprocessors.

Although the other 16-bit machines may have much to recommend them, they are not felt by myself to be as desirable.

This book is oriented towards the person wishing to construct a machine and not simply buy a completed unit. For instance, Hewlett-Packard MC2 is used by Hewlett-Packard and is not, at this time, available to anyone else.

The LSI-11 is a multichip system, already designed, and is not available as a separate chip set. This makes sense if we remember that it is meant to duplicate a PDP-11 as a whole and variations would defeat the original design purposes.

Although the 9440 and the microNOVA are available as separate chips and chip sets, they are meant to exactly duplicate the NOVA system by Data General.

WHY THE 9900?

The TI 9900 was chosen for this book for several reasons; it is an LSI minicomputer rather than a microcomputer chip (microprocessor) in the usual sense of the word. This means that, for the hobbyist or professional, the instruction set and architecture are simple and clean, with little to interfere with designing hardware or software.

The minimum system (see Chapter 4 for a block diagram) is not significantly more expensive than a minimum system using other processors, and may even be less expensive, particularly when compared to other 16-bit processors.

The 9900 is a 16-bit machine with byte addressing and a general register bank (16 registers); it is a 64-pin chip with separate lines for data and addresses, making complex interfaces unnecessary; and it does not require the use of complex memory systems to operate, allowing easy mixing of different memories.

The family of 9900 chips is complete, allowing powerful systems to be designed with ease. There exists currently a version of the TMS9900, called the TMS9980, which can use 8-bit modules and is totally software compatible with the 9900.

The 9900, while still young in terms of software, has most of the key software already available, such as:

1) COBAL—full ANSI COBOL compiler
2) FORTRAN—a re-entrant, full ANSI/ISO compiler
3) A real-time multiprogramming, time-sharing operating system with all the bells and whistles.
4) BASIC—A time-sharing BASIC

The 9900 is available as a one-card computer called the 990/4, as a one-card computer with on-board RAM and ROM called the 990-100M, a TTL version with memory mapping to two-million bytes, called the 990/10. There also exists an I^2L version, with higher speed and pin compatibility termed the IBP-9900. There is the 9980 (8-bit compatible) version of the 990-100M called the 990-180M. And of course the TMS9900, TMS9980, and the IBP9900 are all available as separate chips, along with the rest of the family chips.

All in all I feel that the TMS9900 (or the IBP9900), as a personal computer, is an excellent choice.

WHAT IS IN THIS BOOK

The 9900 chip itself is obviously covered in detail, since this is the central processing unit, the very nucleus of the computer system.

The 9901 is a programmable systems interface, which provides the 9900 with an interval timer, an event timer, up to 16 I/O ports, and up to 15 interrupt input lines.

The 9902 is an asynchronous communication controller (ACC), which allows interfacing the 9900 to such devices as teletypewriters of all kinds, CRT terminals, hard-copy terminals, paper tape readers, and punches and cassette tape interfaces.

The 9904 is a clock generator which generates all the synchronization signals for the 9900, the 9901, etc.

The 9903 is a synchronous communication controller which eliminates the need for software for the protocols, such as binary synchronous (often called bi-synch), synchronous data link control (usually SDLC), and almost all other synchronous protocols, with the link synchronization and control handled by this chip, the 9903.

The TMS9900 Processor Chip

2

The TMS9900 is a single IC in a 64-pin dual inline package. This package (Fig. 2-1) is larger than the more familiar 8-bit microprocessor chips. The 9900 is 3.2 inches long, and the two rows of pins are 0.900 inch apart rather than the 0.600 inch spacing used in 40-pin packages. Adjacent pin spacing is the familiar 0.010 inch. Pin number 1 is identified by an index dot between Pins 1 and 2.

The chip is produced by N-channel silicon-gate MOS technology, and requires three power supplies for its operation. The recommended levels for these supplies are −5, +5, and +12 VDC. Under typical conditions, the chip draws 50 ma from the +5 VDC supply 75 ma is rated maximum), 100 microamps from the −5 VDC rail 1 ma maximum), and 25 ma from the +12 VDC source (45 ma maximum).

All signal levels (except for the four clock signals), both input and output, are compatible with TTL logic. The clock signals must not be lower than +3 V at their positive points, and TTL guarantees only a +2.4-volt level for a HI signal. If the recommended TIM9904 clock chip is used to provide the clock signals you will have no problem; TTL normally provides adequate drive, but this is not guaranteed.

Maximum clock frequency is 3 MHz, and four non-overlapping phases must be supplied. The 9904 circuit uses a 48-MHz crystal, or a 12-MHz external oscillator, to provide these requirements. Fig.

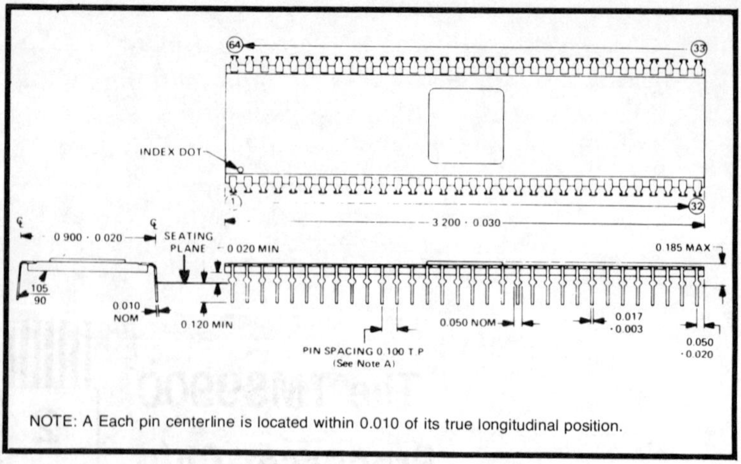

Fig. 2-1. The 64-pin dual inline package of the TMS9900 is larger than the more familiar 40-pin DIP configuration used by 8-bit microprocessors. Added 24 pins make possible more system interconnections. (Courtesy of Texas Instruments)

2-2 shows clock signal timing requirements. The times shown are for maximum-frequency operation. For operation at slower speeds, the duration of individual phases may be extended but the 5-ns guard times between signals should remain unchanged.

Input lines to the TMS9900 all have high impedance to minimize loading on signal sources. Outputs are all capable of driving two

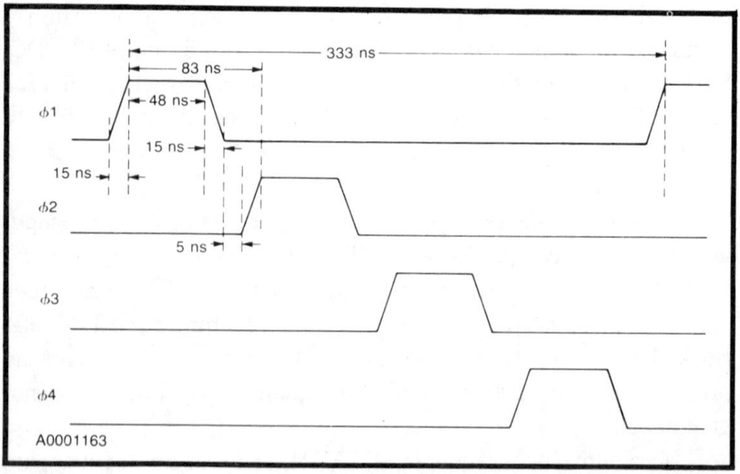

Fig. 2-2. Clock waveforms required by TMS9900 when operating at maximum 3-MHz frequency are shown here. Dead space of 5 ns between phases is essential to proper operation of processor. (Courtesy of Texas Instruments)

standard TTL inputs each, and no pull-up resistors are necessary. Most standard memory devices can be connected directly to the 9900 without intervening buffers. If an external circuit imposes more than the equivalent of two TTL loads (that is, requires more than 3.2 ma of driving signal), buffering is required.

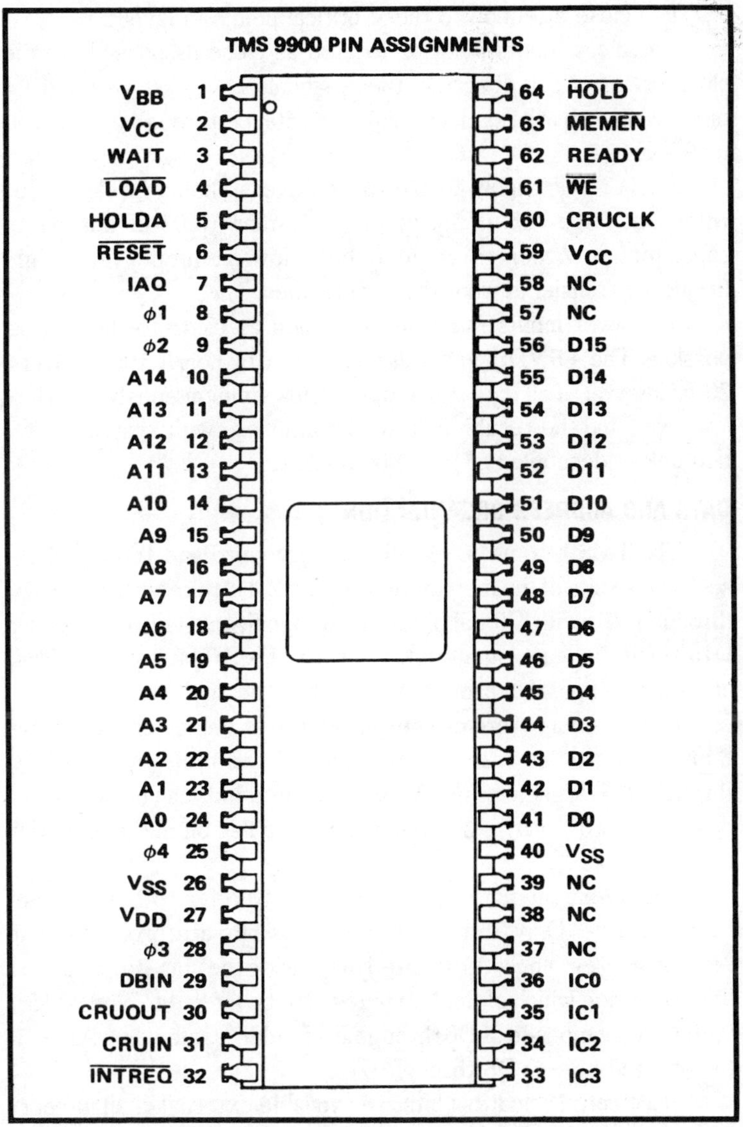

Fig. 2-3. Pin connections for processor chip are grouped by function to simplify PWA card layout. (Courtesy of Texas Instruments)

Pin assignments of the TMS9900 (Fig. 2-3) were made to simplify the layout of a circuit board, by grouping related signals into sets and assigning each set to adjacent pins. Thus all signals of the data bus are together, and so forth. This permits shorter conductor runs and more compact circuit board layout.

Pay close attention to these critical points in layout:

The clock inputs must be located as close as possible to the clock driver circuit, because these signals have fast rise and fall times while driving relatively high capacitance through a wide voltage swing.

The 12-volt supply to the clock drivers should be decoupled with both large (15-uf minimum) and small (0.05-uf maximum) capacitors in order to remove both low-frequency and high-frequency transients from the supply lines.

All power inputs must be decoupled as close to the chip as possible. The +5 VDC power drain can vary by nearly 100 ma over a 20-ns interval, if all data and address lines simultaneously switch to low level, and the resulting spike can interfere with system operation unless decoupled at the 9900 socket.

DATA AND ADDRESS ORGANIZATION

The TMS9900 uses a 16-bit memory word and 16-bit addresses. The 16 bits of the memory word (Fig. 2-4) are referred to as DO through D15, with D0 being the most significant (leftmost) bit and D15 being the least significant. Similarly, the 16 bits of an address are referred to as A0 through A15, with A0 being most significant.

Each memory word can be considered as being made up of two 8-bit bytes. In this case, D0 through D7 form one byte, and D8 through D15 form the other. Most data operations can be performed on either words or bytes, depending upon a flag bit in the operation command code.

The 16-bit memory addresses actually refer to bytes rather than to words. Only 15 of the 16 address bits are brought out to external address lines; A15 is used only inside the chip, to signify to a byte operation which of the two bytes is to be affected. When A15 is 0, the byte composed of D0 through D7 is addressed; when A15 is 1, the affected byte is D8 through D15.

Since only 15 address bits are available externally, all memory addresses involve full 16-bit words, and are on even-byte boundaries. That is, memory location 0001 does not exist; the system

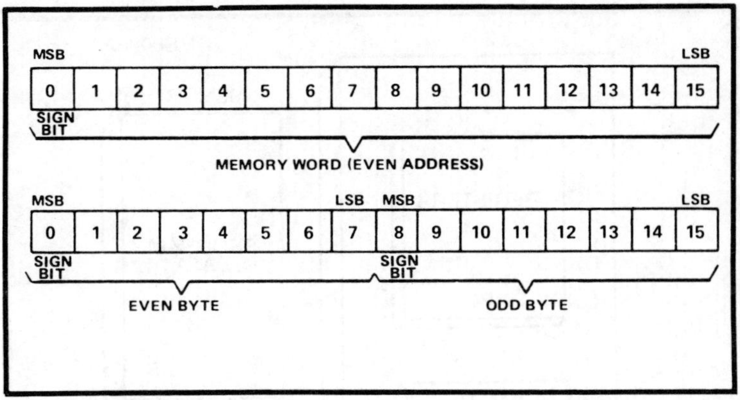

Fig. 2-4. Bit designations which memory word are as shown at top here. Bytes of word are as shown below. (Courtesy of Texas Instruments)

steps from 0000 to 0002, then to 0004, and so forth. Thus the memory space directly addressible is 32,768 words, and any memory transfer moves a full 16-bit word regardless of whether one or both its bytes are to be modified.

INTERNAL ORGANIZATION

The advanced memory-to-memory architecture of the TMS9900 is best described by comparing it to the more conventional register-oriented design exemplified by the popular 8080 microprocessor. Such a chip (Fig. 2-5) contains a number of registers, a program counter, an arithmetic and logic unit (ALU), and a set of status flags. Data may be transferred from register to register, or between register and memory. Most arithmetic and logic operations involve a special register (the accumulator) and either another register, immediate data, or a memory byte.

For controller applications, this is adequate. The control parameters may be kept in the internal registers, and little communication with memory is required for data transfer.

However, when interrupt-driven input-output techniques are employed (which means most of the time, in information processing applications), all of the internal registers must be saved each time an interrupt occurs. Subsequently, at the end of the interrupt service routine, the registers must be restored. This continual saving and restoration of the registers may occupy as much processor time and program space as the interrupt service routine itself.

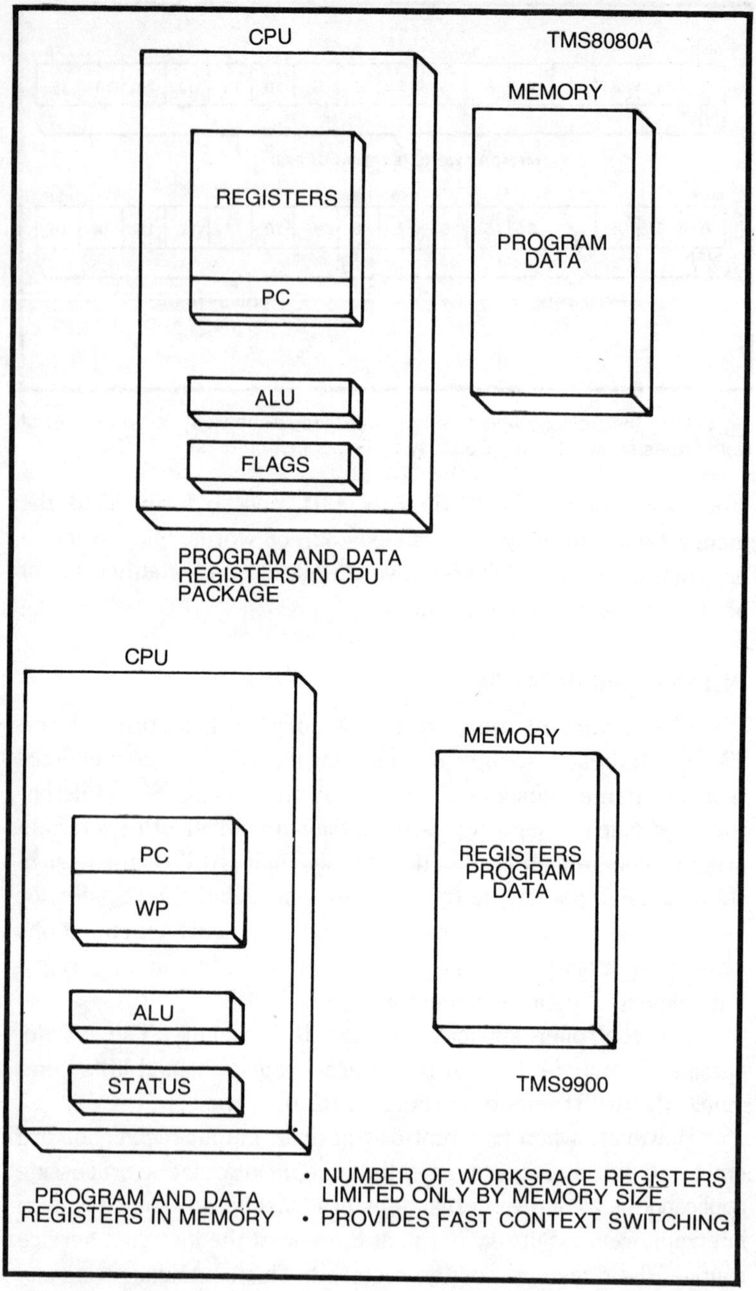

Fig. 2-5. Difference between TMS9900 organization (right) and more conventional approach of 8080 (left) is key to 9900's capability for rapid context switching. (Courtesy of Texas Instruments)

The TMS9900's memory-to-memory design differs in that only three registers are actually contained within the chip, and all three of these are automatically saved or restored as required by single program instructions or interrupt responses. The saving or restoring is called a "context switch."

The three actual registers in the TMS9900 (Fig. 2-5) are the program counter, the status register, and the workspace pointer. The first two of these correspond to their counterparts in the more conventional design; the third is the key to the advantages of the TMS9900.

In addition to the three actual registers, the TMS9900 employs 16 additional "workspace registers." These registers, identified as WR0 through WR15, may be used for the same purposes as any of the additional data registers of the more conventional architecture (with several exceptions). That is, any of the registers may be used as an accumulator or as an address pointer.

The 16 workspace registers (Fig. 2-6) may be located anywhere in memory, and you can have as many sets of them as you like. The only requirements are that the 16 register words in one set be in consecutively addressed locations, and that they not be in read-only memory.

The workspace pointer register points to WR0 in the currently active set of workspace registers; this gives the processor access to all 16 of the registers in the set.

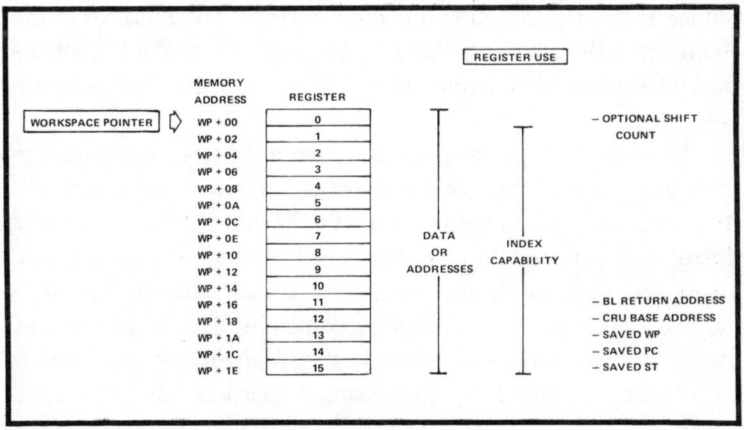

Fig. 2-6. The 16 registers of the 9900 are organized as shown here. All addresses are relative to the workspace pointer. As many sets of registers as desired can be defined. (Courtesy of Texas Instruments)

Of the 16 workspace registers, 10 are available for any application. Three are dedicated to the context-switching operations, but their content may be used or changed by the same commands which apply to the 10 general-usage registers. The remaining three have special uses in certain commands, but again can be changed or used like any other workspace register (with one exception).

Registers WR1 through WR10 are the general-usage registers. Each can be used as an accumulator, a memory pointer, or an index register, depending upon specific bits in the command used to address the register.

The other registers can also be used as accumulators, memory pointers, and (except for WR0) as index registers. Indexing involving WR0 is not allowed.

The registers dedicated to context switching are WR13, WR14, and WR15. When a context switch occurs, the old content of the workspace pointer is stored in WR13 of the new workspace, the old program counter in WR14, and the current content of the status register in WR15. If these three registers are not modified by the program, the context switch can be reversed by reloading WP, PC, and ST from WR13, WR14, and WR15 respectively. This is done by a single command, Return Workspace (RTWP).

Special uses of the remaining registers are as follows: WR0 contains an optional shift count used by all four shift instructions. WR11 contains the return address stored automatically by the Branch and Link (BL) command, which can be used to call a subroutine without performing a context switch. To return from the subroutine a Branch using WR11 (B 11) is executed. WR12 contains the bit base address for communication-register unit (CRU) operations.

In addition to the workspace-register feature, the memory-to-memory organization of the 9900 has another unusual result. Arithmetic and logical operations are not limited to actions involving the registers; any memory location can be altered, without the need for moving its content into a register to make the change, then moving it back after the change is complete. That is to say, any memory location—not just the workspace registers—can be used as an accumulator, merely by addressing it appropriately in the command.

At first glance, it might appear that this architecture would result in an inordinate number of memory accesses in order to accomplish any program action. In fact, the number of accesses is not significantly larger than with the more conventional register-oriented microprocessor designs, since they too must perform at least one memory access per program instruction in order to fetch the instruction for execution. By reducing the number of program steps which must be accessed, the 9900's design permits more data accesses without penalty.

CONTEXT SWITCHING

The process of switching from one set of registers to another, by switching the pointer to the workspace, is known as context switching. A context switch is performed when the LOAD signal goes low, immediately after the RESET signal returns to high level after being low, when any of the 15 maskable interrupts is recognized and allowed, whenever one of the 16 possible Extended Operation (XOP) commands is executed, whenever a Branch and Load Workspace Pointer (BLWP) command is executed, or when the Return Workspace (RTWP) is executed.

All of these context switches, except that resulting from executing RTWP, are performed in the same manner once the necessity for the context switch is established. External signal lines LOAD and RESET establish the need for their context switches. An allowable interrupt similarly establishes its need. Context switches required by command execution are established by fetching and decoding the command.

Once the need for a context switch is known, the existing workspace pointer and status register are temporarily saved and a new workspace pointer value is obtained from an appropriate memory location. For all context switches except BLWP and RTWP, the location of the new workspace pointer value is built into the 9900 chip (Fig. 2-7). For LOAD the new value is at memory location FFFC (16). For RESET, it is at 0000. For Interrupt 1, it is at 0004, and so forth for the higher-numbered interrupts up to Interrupt 15, at 003C (60 decimal, or 4 times 15). The values for XOP immediately follow those for the interrupts, at memory locations 0040 (XOP 0) through 007C (XOP 15). The value, once obtained, is loaded into the workspace pointer register, which instantly changes the entire program context to reflect the new workspace.

With the new workspace established, the saved value of the status register is stored in new WR15. The content of the program counter register, which has not yet changed, is stored in new WR14. The saved value of the old workspace pointer is stored in WR13, and finally the new value of the program counter is read from the memory location immediately following that from which the new workspace pointer was obtained (FFFE for LOAD, 0002 for RESET, and so forth). Program execution then continues, using the new value of the program counter and the new workspace.

After any of these context switches is accomplished, the first instruction (that addressed by the new program counter) will be executed before any interrupt will be recognized. This permits the interrupt facility to be locked out when desired.

Because the old WP, PC, and ST are pushed into WR13, WR14, and WR15 of the new workspace, it is possible to restore them and thus to restore the exact internal system conditions which existed at the instant the context switch was performed. This is functionally the equivalent of the stack push and pop (or pull) sequences employed by many 8-bit microprocessors. The 9900, however, does everything by a single instruction, rather than requiring an instruction sequence.

Restoring the previously used workspace, PC, and status is accomplished by the RTWP instruction. Its action may also be considered a context switch, but in the reverse direction. The RTWP action is never performed automatically; it always results from the program's fetching and decoding the RTWP command.

When the RTWP command is decoded, the processor fetches the old status from WR15 and stores it in the status register. Next, it restores the program counter from WR14. Then it restores the workspace pointer from WR13. Note that the values of ST, PC, and WP which existed when the command was decoded have been lost; none of them are necessary any longer. Finally, the restored program counter content is loaded onto the memory address lines and the next instruction is taken from the location thus addressed. Unlike the other context switches, the interrupt facility remains active when RTWP is executed (unless disabled by the restored interrupt mask in the status register).

INTERRUPTS

The TMS9900 provides 16 interrupts, together with LOAD and RESET pins. Interrupt 0 and RESET accomplish the same actions.

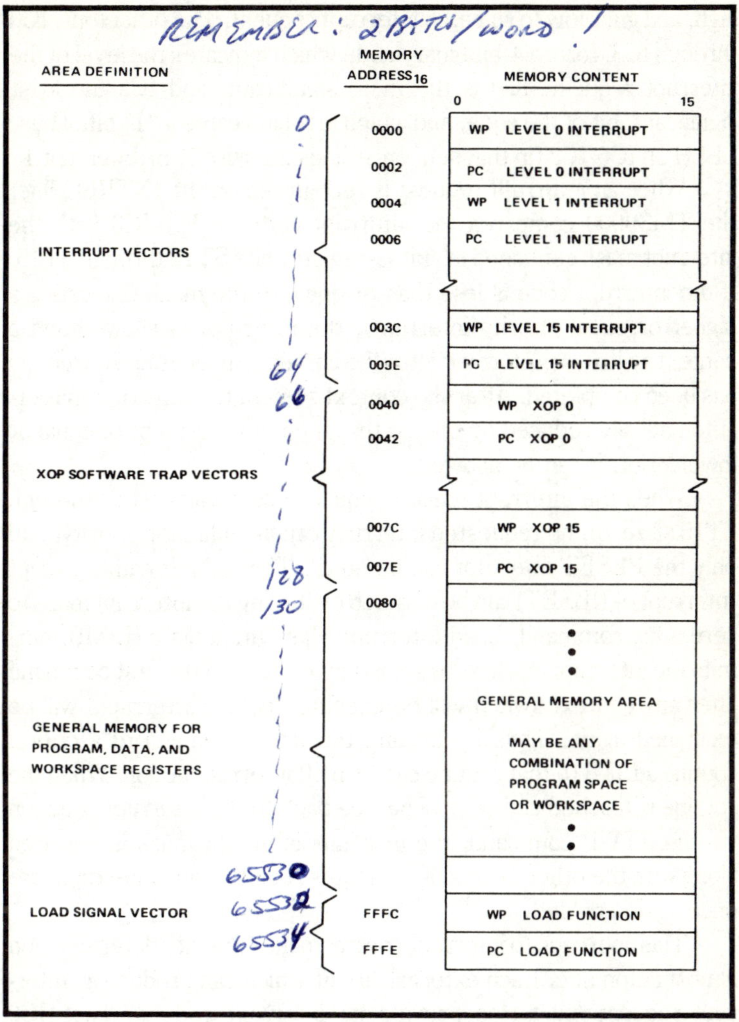

Fig. 2-7. Memory locations 0000 through 007E, plus FFFC and FFFE, are dedicated to special uses as shown in this memory map. All other addresses are free for general use. (Courtesy of TI)

Interrupt priority is established by the number of the interrupt. Interrupt 15 has lowest priority, and Interrupt 0 or RESET the highest. Interrupt 0 cannot be masked; the remaining 15 are automatically masked in such a way that no interrupt of lower priority will be accepted while any interrupt is being serviced.

The interrupt system uses five lines. One, INTREQ, signals the TMS9900 that an interrupt is requested. This line is normally high, and goes low to signal an interrupt request. The other four, IC0 through IC3, form a 4-bit binary code which indicates the level of the interrupt request. IC0 is the most significant, and IC3 the least significant, bit of the code, and a high level indicates a "1" bit. Thus, LLLH on IC0-IC3 (in that sequence) indicates 0001, or Interrupt 1.

When an interrupt request is recognized on the INTREQ line, the TMS9900 compares the interrupt code on IC0-IC3 with the interrupt mask contained in status-register bits ST12 through ST15. If the interrupt code is less than or equal to the mask (indicating a higher or equal priority interrupt), the interrupt is allowed and a context switch is performed after the currently executing instruction has been completed. After the context switch, the interrupt mask is automatically reduced by one so that no other interrupt of equal or lower priority can be allowed.

When the interrupt mask is equal to zero (bits ST12 through ST15 all zero), no requested interrupt can be of higher priority, and only the RESET interrupt can be equal. Thus all interrupts except Interrupt 0 (RESET) can be disabled by forcing the interrupt mask to zero. One command, Load Interrupt Mask Immediate (LIMI), permits the interrupt mask to be set to any value, and the first command after any context switch will be executed before interrupts will be examined again. Thus by making the first command of a critical routine a LIMI 0, that routine can turn off interrupt action. When the routine is finished and control passes back to the interrupted action via the RTWP command, the previous interrupt mask is restored along with the other 12 bits of the status register, and interrupts are once again enabled.

This approach to interrupt control makes priority determination almost automatic. Each external circuit which can produce an interrupt request must also provide its interrupt code on lines IC0 through IC3. If each device has a separate code, no additional hardware is necessary to determine which device requires service or if response is permissible. Most systems can operate with no more than 15 different interrupts. Should more prove necessary, several devices can be assigned the same code and the interrupt service routine can then interrogate all of them to determine which requires service. Alternatively, external hardware can be added to sort out priorities so that the 9900 sees only one of 15 requests, but each request could have originated from any of several different circuits.

INPUT/OUTPUT TECHNIQUES

Any or all of three widely different techniques may be used for input/output data transfers between the TMS9900 processor and memory on one side, and the external world on the other. The three techniques (Fig. 2-8) are direct memory access (DMA), memory-mapped I/O, and the communications-register unit (CRU) capability.

DMA provides direct transfer of data between the peripheral devices and memory, without involving the processor at all (except to guarantee that the processor does not attempt to access memory at the same time). With many processors, this is the cleanest way to transfer data, but it always requires some external hardware to control the DMA activity and to assure that both the processor and the peripheral device wait their proper turns for memory access. Because of its complexity, DMA I/O is outside the scope of this volume.

Memory-mapped I/O assigns memory addresses to the various peripheral ports, and "reads" from or "writes" to the peripheral port just as though it were actual memory. This approach makes at least one memory location per peripheral device unavailable for actual data storage, but nevertheless is a popular technique. Several 8-bit microprocessors (notably, the 6500 and 6800 families) use memory-mapped I/O to meet all their requirements. Again, memory-mapped I/O is outside the scope of this volume, because

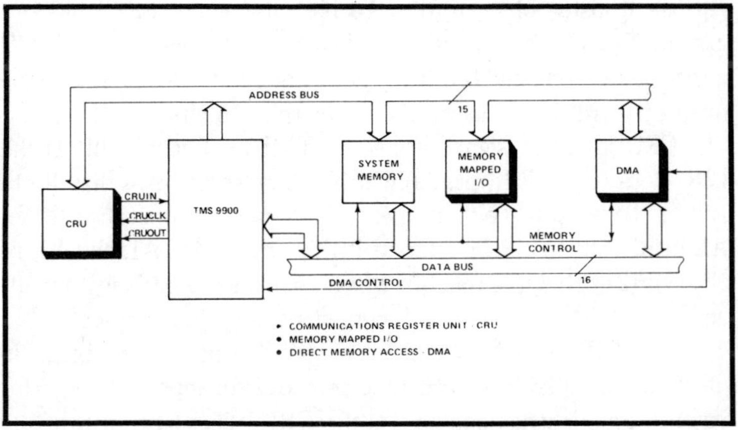

Fig. 2-8. These three types of input/output techniques may be used with the 9900. Only the CRU capability is unique to the 9900. (Courtesy of Texas Instruments)

the technique used depends entirely upon the specific peripheral involved.

The final technique, the CRU capability, is unique to the TMS9900 family and is an extension of the idea used for direct accumulator I/O in such processors as the 8080.

A communications register unit is defined in the 9900 system as any external unit making use of the processor's CRU capability. This capability takes the form of three dedicated I/O pins (CRUIN, CRUOUT, and CRUCLK), 12 bits (A3 through A13) of the address bus, and five processor instructions which permit the program to set, reset, or test any of 4096 addressable bits in the external device, and to move data between memory and CRU data fields.

While the capability provides 12 bits of CRU address, making it possible to uniquely address up to 4096 bits in the CRU, any specific device used as a CRU need not have all these bits present. A single-bit device such as a flip-flop could be used as a CRU. In a more practical vein, the TMS9901, 9902, and 9903 peripherals are all intended to be used as CRU's. If you prefer, any type of peripheral controller can be turned into a CRU by providing the proper interface to make it compatible with the 9900's CRU-oriented commands and bit addressing.

CRU INTERFACING

The CRU interface is a dedicated serial I/O capability which permits transfer of from 1 to 16 bits at a time. Since bits are individually addressed, no masking instructions are necessary in I/O service programs, and I/O fields need not be identical in size to the memory word (but must be no longer than 16 bits).

CRU interface signals from the TMS9900 consist of (1) the CRU clock (CRUCLK, pin 60) which, when high, means that the 15 address lines contain either an externally decoded operation (if A0, A1, or A2 is high) or a bit address in the CRU (if A0, A1, and A2 are all low); (2) CRUOUT (pin 30) which contains the bit being output; and (3) CRUIN (pin 31) which contains the bit being input.

The CRU can be considered to be a pair of addressable memories of 4096 bits each (one memory for input, and one for output). Five instructions access the CRU. They are:

- Test Bit (TB), which allows reading any single bit in the CRU;

- Set Bit to One (SBO) and
- Set Bit to Zero (SBZ), which allow altering one bit in the CRU; and
- Load Communications Register (LDCR) and
- Store Communications Register (STCR), which allow altering or reading up to 16 bits at a time via a multi-bit CRU data transfer.

Each of these five instructions first causes the address of a single bit in the CRU address space to be formed as shown in Fig. 2-9 by adding a displacement value (contained in the instruction) to the CRU base address (contained in WR12), then places the resulting bit address on address lines A3 through A14 while forcing A0, A1, and A2 to 000. The bit appears on either CRUIN (for TB or STCR) or CRUOUT (for SBO, SBZ, or LDCR), strobed by CRUCLK.

The three single-bit commands operate explicitly; TB places the received bit value into ST2, where it may be tested by a subsequent JEQ or JNE command. If the bit value was 1, the EQUAL condition is set. SBO and SBZ set the CRU bit to 1 and 0, respectively.

Only one bit per machine cycle is processed by any of the CRU commands. Multi-bit commands LDCR and STCR perform as many cycles as necessary to transfer the specified number of bits, chang-

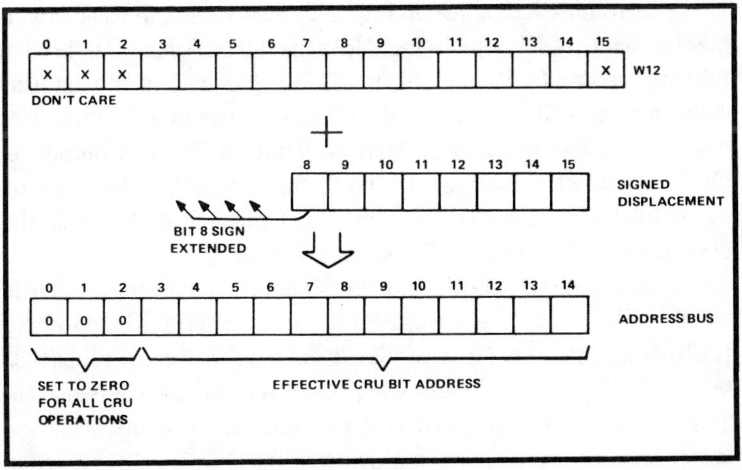

Fig. 2-9. The CRU address placed on the address bus (bottom) is developed by adding an 8-bit signed displacement contained in the I/O command itself (center) to the CRU base address held in workspace register 12 (top). This operation is repeated for each addressed bit. (Courtesy of Texas Instruments)

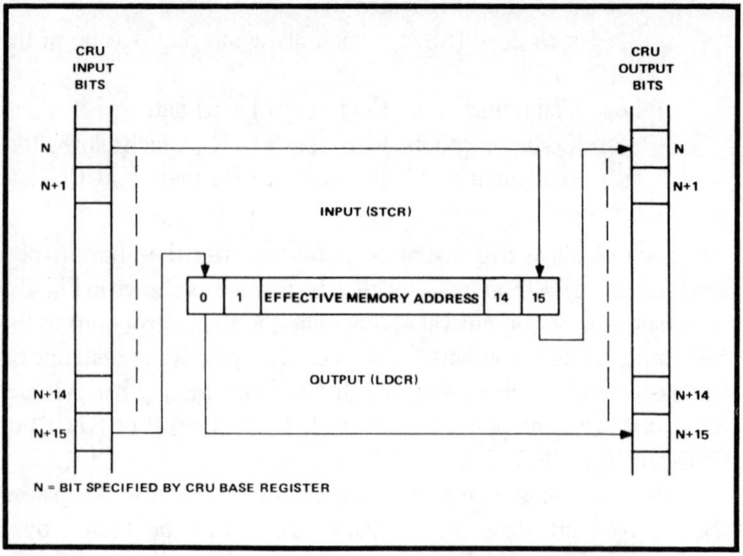

Fig. 2-10. Multi-bit CRU data transfers by the LDCR and STCR commands operate as shown here. On input (STCR), the bit having the lowest CRU address moves into the rightmost bit of the addressed memory word. On output (LDCR), similarly, the rightmost bit goes to the lowest CRU address. (Courtesy of Texas Instruments)

ing the bit address after each cycle. Each bit is moved between processor and CRU as shown in Fig. 2-10.

The 16-bit CRU shown in Fig. 2-11 illustrates the basic principles involved in CRU interfacing. Note that address lines A0 through A10 are ignored by this circuit; it will interpret any of the external commands as a CRU action, and each of its 16 input and output bits has 256 possible addresses. That is, input bit IN0 and output bit OUT0 can be addressed as CRU bit 0, bit 16, bit 32, and so forth up to bit 4080. Whenever address lines A11 through A14 contain the 0000 pattern, IN0 and OUT0 are addressed.

The TMS9901, 9902, and 9903 support chips (discussed in detail in Chapter 3) are designed for use with the CRU interface. Each of them has only 5 address-line inputs, so each chip occupies 32 bits of the 4096-bit CRU memory space. Each of these chips also has a Chip Enable (CE) input to permit the other seven address lines to select one of several chips in a system.

If only one CRU device is to be used, the multiple-address approach (simply grounding the CE line) would be enough. However, let us suppose that we wish to connect 8 devices on the CRU interface. We can divide the CRU address signal as follows;

1) 9901 for interrupts and interval timer, addressesd as bits 0-31
2) 9902 for master terminal, addresses 32-63
3) Four 9902s for remote terminals, modems, addresses
64-95
96-127
128-159
160-191
4) 9903 for a BI-SYNC terminal addresses 192-223
5) 9903 for an SDLC terminal addresses 224-255

The circuit as shown in Fig. 2-12 would be used. This circuit uses an 74LS138 3-to-8 decoder. Line Z comes from the CRU clock.

Should we wish to further expand the system, we could use Fig. 2-13 to increase the number of circuits to 64. This requires 9 74LS138 decoders. Figure 2-14 shows decoding for your system up to 128 devices, allowing up to 127 terminals to be connected to such a system. This circuit requires 36 74LS138 decoders and some TTL circuitry.

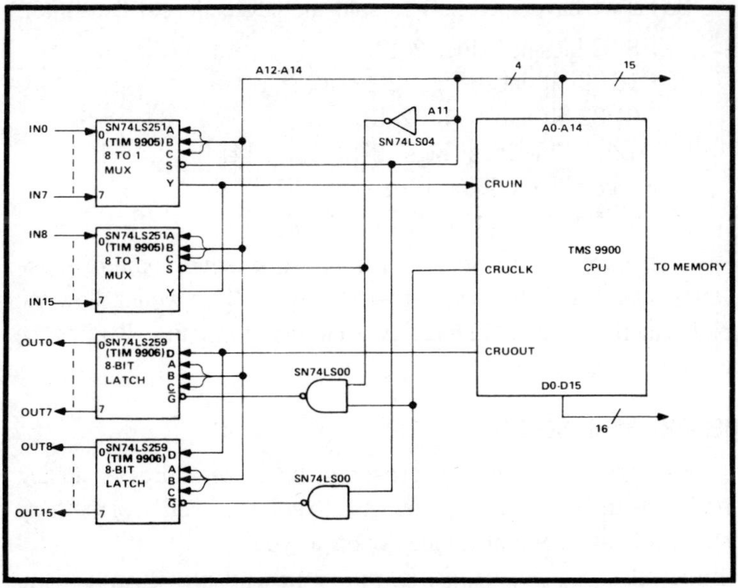

Fig. 2-11. This 16-bit CRU can be constructed with only 5 IC chips, since one-quarter of a 74LS00 can be used instead of the 74LS04. It may be adequate for small systems. (Courtesy of Texas Instruments)

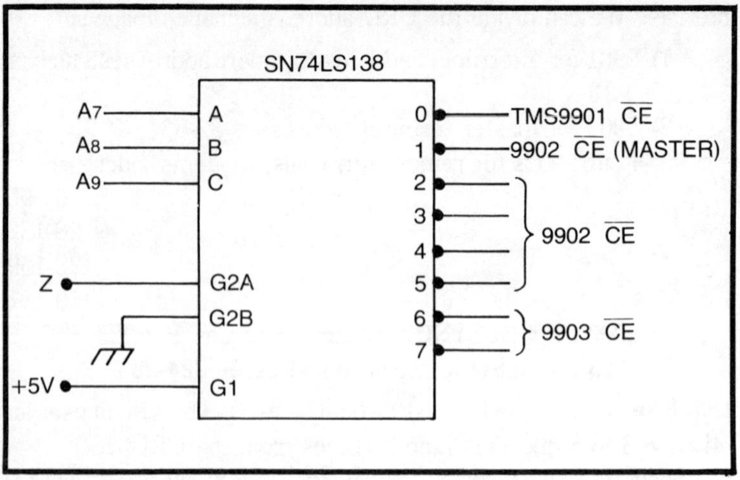

Fig. 2-12. This 3-to-8 decoder can be used to select one of eight CRU devices.

Should a chip require the use of more than 32 bits of the CRU, Fig. 2-15 shows a technique to tie two select lines together. By tying two lines together we allow up to 64 CRU bits to be addressed as a group. To split a 32 bit group into two 16 bit groups, use Fig. 2-16.

So far we have seen how to split the CRU address lines into:

A) 8 32-bit lines (Fig. 2-12)
B) 16 32-bit lines (Figs. 2-12 and 2-14)
C) 64 32-bit lines (Fig. 2-13)
D) 128 32-bit lines (Figs. 2-13 and 2-14)
E) recombined 64-bit lines (Fig. 2-15)
F) split-pair 16-bit lines (Fig. 2-16)

There are, of course, other ways to achieve some of these results. One way is to use a 4-to-16 decoder. This would allow the combination of Fig. 2-14 plus two circuits from Fig. 2-12 to be replaced by one circuit.

MEMORY BANK SELECTION

Memory system design presents the same address-mapping problem as the CRU. Should you wish to select a section of memory you would have several choices open to you:

- Select logic as shown in Fig. 2-17 will allow selecting any group of 4K words of storage, up to the maximum of 32K words.

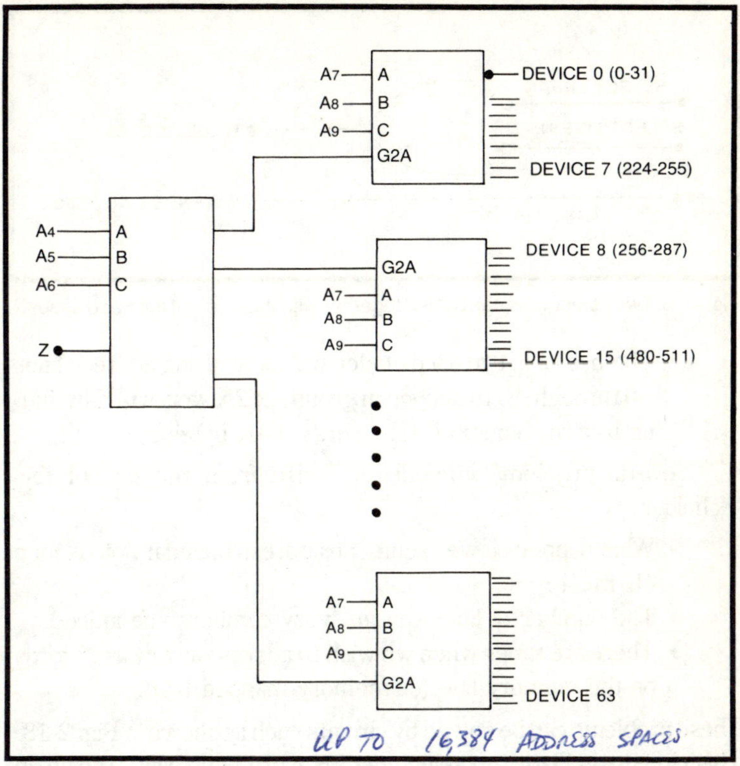

Fig. 2-13. By increasing the number of decoders to 9, we can handle up to 64 different devices.

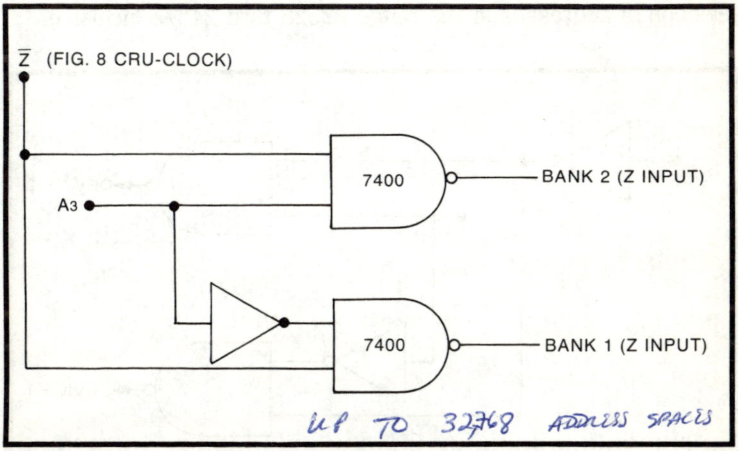

Fig. 2-14. For a maximum system we can use this circuit with 36 decoders and associated logic to select one of 128 CRU devices.

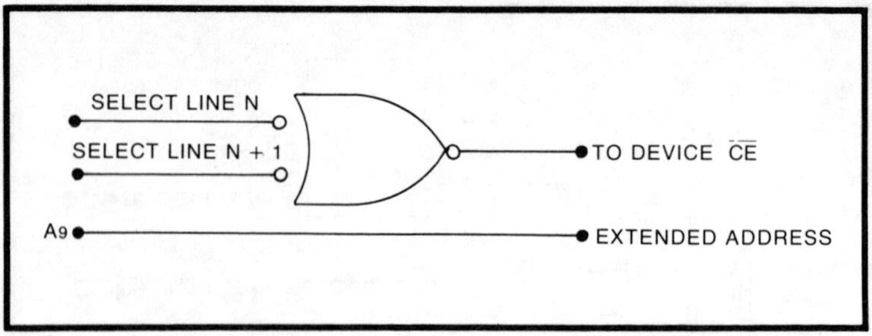

Fig. 2-15. Two select lines can be tied together with this circuit if the need arises.

- The use of a 4-to-16 decoder will allow using address lines A0 through A3 to decode in groups of 2K words (4K bytes), up to a maximum of 32K words (64K bytes).

Several problems immediately arise from the use of this technique.

- What happens if we require an address boundary of 1K for a 4K range?
- The number of lines can get very cumbersome indeed.
- There are times when we wish to address as few as 2 words on the memory line (or memory mapped I/O).

These problems can be solved by circuits such as shown in Fig. 2-18. This circuit can be set to select any 2K word boundary. Adding an extra section would allow us to select any 1k word boundary. As an example: closing switches A01, A12, A21 and A31 would cause selection of addresses in the range 22528 thru 24575 inclusive.

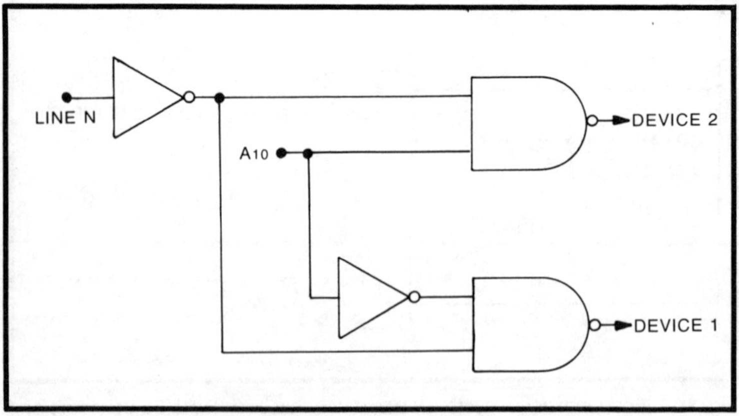

Fig. 2-16. This circuit can split a 32-bit group into two 16-bit groups.

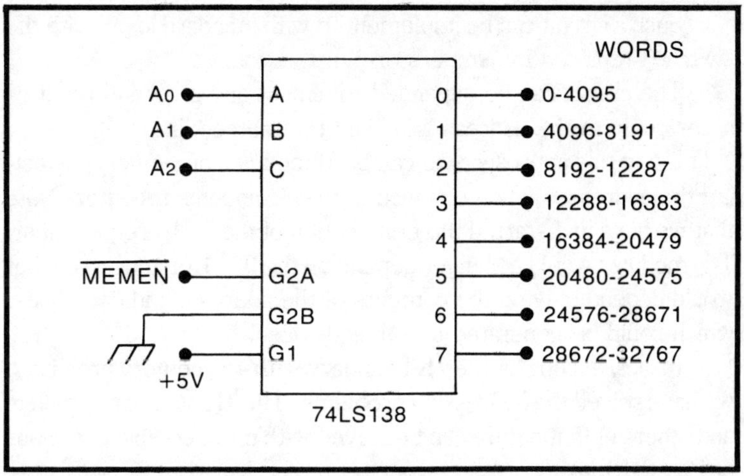

Fig. 2-17. A 3-to-8 decoder allows selection of any single 4K-word block of memory, up to the maximum 32K of a 9900 system.

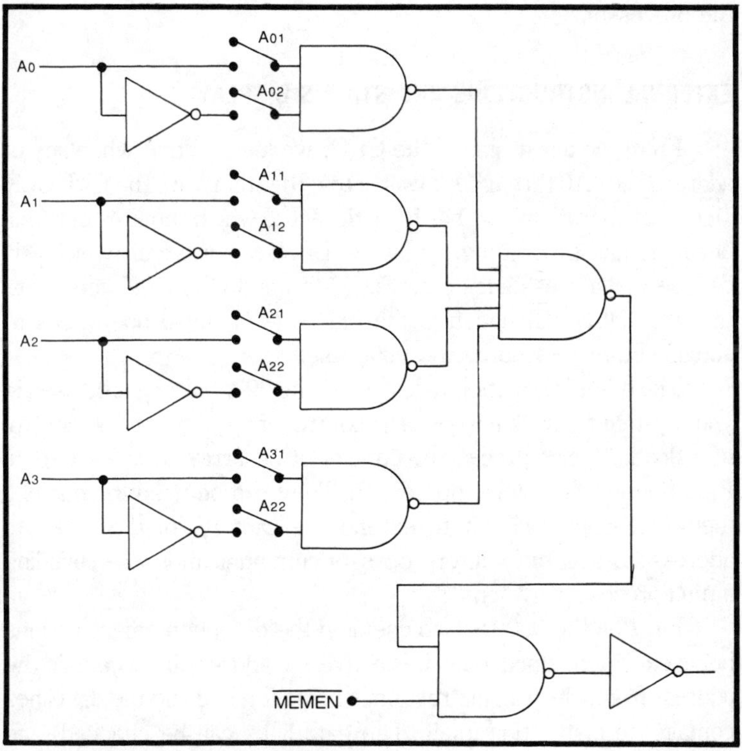

Fig. 2-18. This circuit can be used to select memory on any 2K boundary rather than the 4K boundaries offered by Fig. 2-17.

Such a circuit can be implemented with standard logic, with the switches replaced by jumpers or plugs.

The circuit can be expanded to almost any level and requires access only to the address lines and the memen line.

Using this approach, we can build modules of memory, selecting the addresses when connecting these modules together. Note that we have just started the first section of the DMA requirement. The modules would no longer depend on the 9900 for addresses, but would depend only on the contents of the address (and data) lines, which could be generated by other devices.

In fact, except for the 1K boundary with 4K memory problems, we have solved the addressing problems. The 1K boundary problem and others of that nature can be solved with more complex versions of Fig. 2-18.

For CRU utilization it is recommended that the multiline decoder approach be used, since these devices are more closely tied to the processor.

EXTERNAL INSTRUCTIONS AND STATUS DISPLAY

From the discussion of the CRU, we learned that when any of address lines A0 through A2 was active together with the CRUCLK signal, an operation code has been detected which requires external decoding and processing. Figure 2-19 shows a circuit which will decode the address lines (see Fig. 2-20) and CRUCLK line. Note that the IDLE instruction is the only one of these operations to actually be processed by the 9900 itself.

The other instructions are used in the 990, but might be used in your system for such purposes as control of interval timers, control of a floating point processor, control of an array processor, or a Fast-Fourier Transform processor. They can be used to control a memory mapping circuit to extend the capacity of the 9900, to address storage, or for interprocessor communication when building a multiprocessor system.

Pin 7 on the 9900 is also useful in the detection of instructions being executed, since when it is active the address lines contain the address from which an instruction is being fetched and the data lines contain the instruction itself. The data lines can be checked, and special instructions could be externally executed or the instruction could force an interrupt.

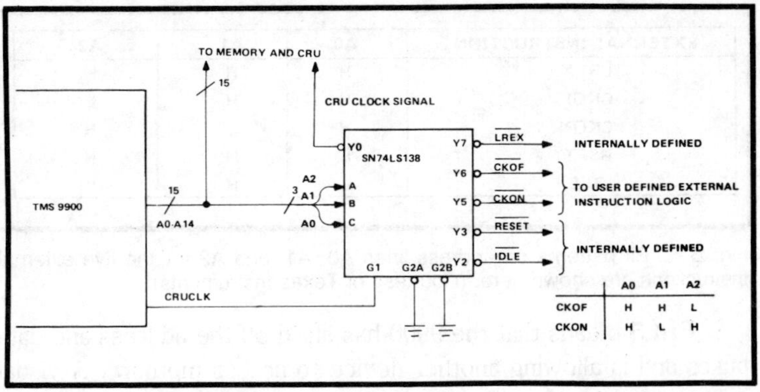

Fig. 2-19. The external instruction decode logic shown here makes it possible to use customized instructions, and also offers insurance against faulty CRU operation. (Courtesy of Texas Instruments)

The designer could force new instructions (such as floating point or decimal instructions) into the machine by the use of memory waits and external execution. Designing such an extension is outside the scope of this book. However I can show you an excellent use for these signals as indicators of the processor state at any time. The following pins are probed on the processor and related circuits:

- The IDLE and RESET signals from Fig. 2-19 as well as the output CRU clock signal. These are pins Y2, Y3, and Y0 respectively on the SN74LS138.
- Pins 7, 61 (write enable), and 63 (memory enable) on the 9900.

The resultant pinout of Fig. 2-21 can be connected to an LED readout to produce a front panel showing processor status. Note that pins 32, 5, and 3 of the 9900 are also shown. The basic reasons for connecting these additional pins to an indicator are:

Pin 32. This output Fig. 2-9, under typical conditions, would usually result in a very brief, almost invisible flash of light. However, it is possible for a more visible indication to occur as follows:

1. Looping in an interrupt routine would mean that the lower priority interrupts are being held, and the light would remain on. See Fig. 2-22 for a list of interrupt priorities.
2. Heavy interrupt rates can cause stacking of the interrupts and result in a visual indication of the interrupt rate. The brighter the light, the higher the rate.

EXTERNAL INSTRUCTION	A0	A1	A2
LREX	H	H	H
CKOF	H	H	L
CKON	H	L	H
RSET	L	H	H
IDLE	L	H	L

Fig. 2-20. Bit patterns on address lines A0, A1, and A2 for the five external instructions are shown here. (Courtesy of Texas Instruments)

Pin 5 means that the 9900 has lifted off the address and data buses and is allowing another device to access memory. A visual indicator would show how much of the time (by brightness) is being used by external devices on the line.

Pin 3 would have meaning, if probed with a lamp indicator, only if mixed speed memories were used. Whenever this pin is active, the TMS9900 must wait for memory. The brightness of the lamp would indicate when a slow section of storage was being accessed.

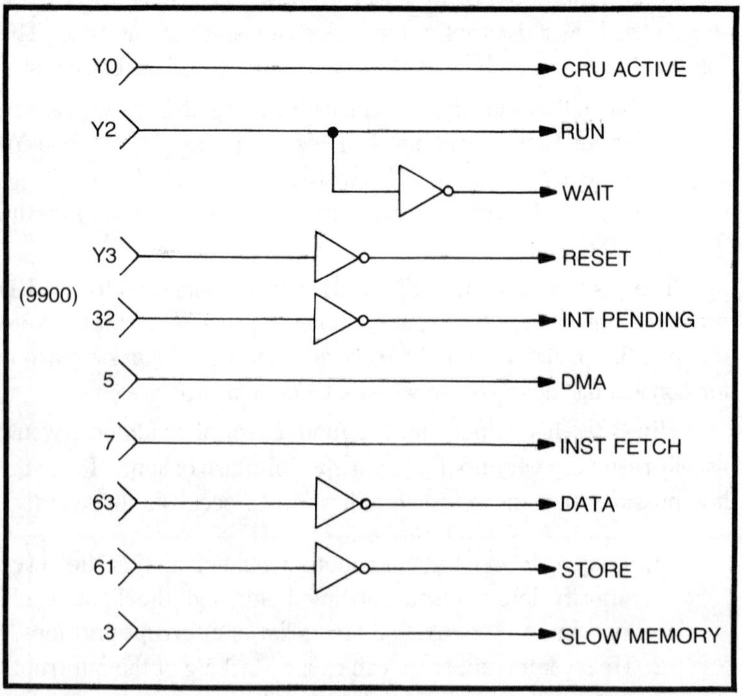

Fig. 2-21. Connecting indicators as shown here provides an informative front-panel display for a 9900 system. See text for full use of the information displayed.

Interrupt Level	Vector Location (Memory Address In Hex)	Device Assignment	Interrupt Mask Values To Enable Respective Interrupts (ST12 thru ST15)	Interrupt Codes IC0 thru IC3
(Highest priority) 0	00	Reset	0 through F*	0000
1	04	External device	1 through F	0001
2	08	↓	2 through F	0010
3	0C		3 through F	0011
4	10		4 through F	0100
5	14		5 through F	0101
6	18		6 through F	0110
7	1C		7 through F	0111
8	20		8 through F	1000
9	24		9 through F	1001
10	28		A through F	1010
11	2C		B through F	1011
12	30		C through F	1100
13	34		D through F	1101
14	38		E and F	1110
(Lowest priority) 15	3C	External device	F only	1111

* Level 0 can not be disabled.

Fig. 2-22. Interrupt priorities and masking are listed here. (Courtesy of Texas Instruments)

3 TMS9900 Family Support Chips

To support the TMS9900 processor, the manufacturer offers a family of devices.

At this writing, the family includes seven chips in addition to the TMS9900, numbered as 9901 through 9907. The first three are prefixed "TMS" (TMS9901 through TMS9903) and the other four bear a "TIM" prefix.

The four TIM devices are also numbered in the 74000 series, and (with the exception of the TIM9904) are referred to in this volume by their 74000-series identities. These are the devices, their 74000-series numbers, and their functions:

- TMS9901 (no other identity) Programmable System Interface—provides up to 15 single-line interrupt coding and up to 16-bit I/O interfacing.
- TMS9902 (no other identity) Asynchronous Communication Controller—interfaces start-stop serial peripherals.
- TMS9903 (no other identity) Synchronous Communication Controller—interfaces serial peripherals which do not use start-stop protocol.
- TIM9904 (74LS362) Clock Generator—provides required four-phase clock signals for entire system.
- TIM9905 (74LS251) 3-State Octal Multiplexer—accepts signal from one of eight addressed input lines and directs it to single output line.

- TIM9906 (74LS259) Octal Addressable Latch—Latches single-line input signal into one of eight addressed output stores.
- TIM9907 (74148) Priority Encoder—produces 3-bit code to indicate highest-priority input signal which is active.

For the purposes of this volume, only the 9901 through 9904 are discussed, since the TMS9901 includes the functions provided by the remaining three chips. The 9901, in fact, is the functional equivalent of two each of the other three chips, although not all this capability can be used at the same time.

TMS9901 PROGRAMMABLE SYSTEM INTERFACE

The TMS9901 is a standard 40-pin DIP device (Fig. 3-1) which has 9 CRU-interface lines which communicate with the 9900, 5 interrupt-interface lines which also communicate with the 9900, 22 system-directed lines, a reset pin, two power pins, and a clock input.

The CRU-interface lines are CRUOUT (pin 2), CRUCLK (pin 3), CRUIN (pin 4), Address Select lines S0 through S4, (pins 39, 36, 35, 25, and 24), and Chip Enable (pin 5). The interrupt-interface lines are INTREQ (pin 11) and IC0 through IC3 (pins 15, 14, 13, and 12). The 22 system-directed lines are divided into three buffer

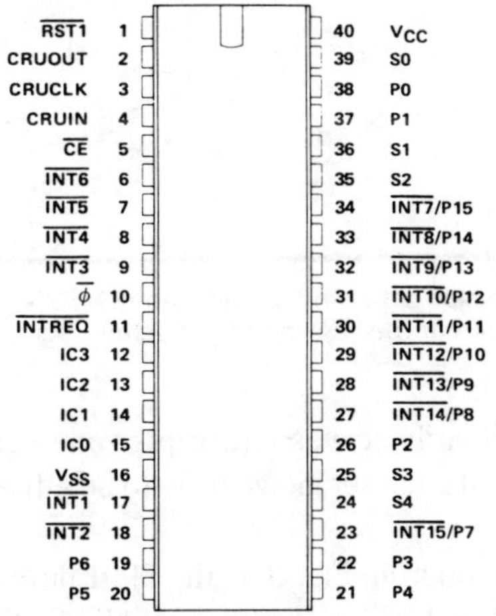

Fig. 3-1. The TMS9901 is supplied in a 40-pin DIP. These are the pin assignments. (Courtesy of Texas Instruments)

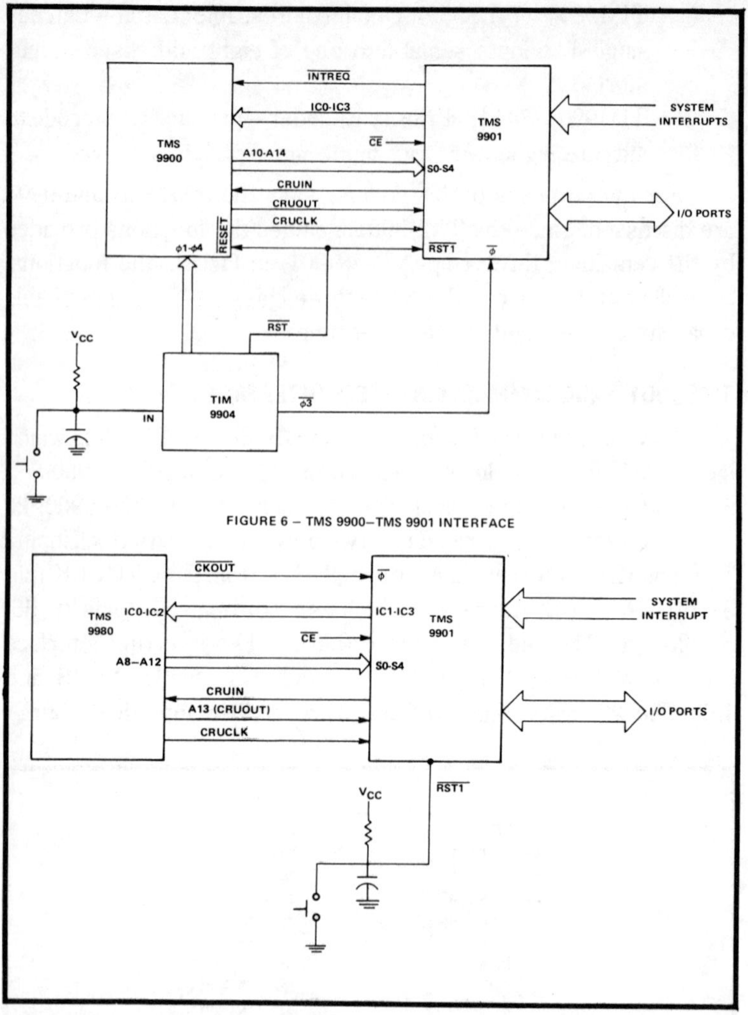

Fig. 3-2. Interconnection between TMS9901 and TMS9900 can be as simple as this. Note that 9904 can be replaced by discrete logic. (Courtesy of Texas Instruments)

groups. One primarily serves interrupts, one serves only as I/O, and one can have its bits set individually to be either interrupt or I/O functions.

As can be seen from Fig. 3-2, the 9901 directly couples to the 9900; it uses only a decoder circuit to enable the CRU interface (the decoder circuit consists of the circuit shown in Fig. 2-19, to obtain the CRU clocking pulse and a comparator circuit to generate a Chip

Enable when address lines A3 through A9 inclusive contain the correct value). This chip-enable circuit must be active low and will result in making the 9901 relocatable from the zero position, as well as allowing multiple 9901 chips to be used.

The 9901 consists of three buffer groups: buffer group one (normally used for interrupts) consists of six input-output buffers (pins 9, through 17, and 18). They can also be used as input buffers, allowing up to 22 lines to be used as input.

Buffer group two, (pins 23 and 27 through 34) consists of nine bidirectional buffers which can be individually set to behave as either I/O ports or interrupt ports. If a port is predisabled as an interrupt port, then it can be used as an I/O port in safety.

Buffer group three behaves as a series of 1-bit I/O ports (pins 19 through 22, 26, 37, and 38).

Also included in the 9901 are a real-time clock, which can be controlled and read through the use of CRU commands; a register mask, holding the interrupt masks; a prioritizer and encoder, which converts 15-line code to 4 with latching to generate the interrupt codes; and CRU logic to control the above devices.

The 9901 allows the 9900 to have additional features. One is a true real-time clock, which has an interrupt priority of 3 (see Fig. 3-3). This clock, using the master clock that is usually crystal controlled, can behave either as an interval timer, generating inter-

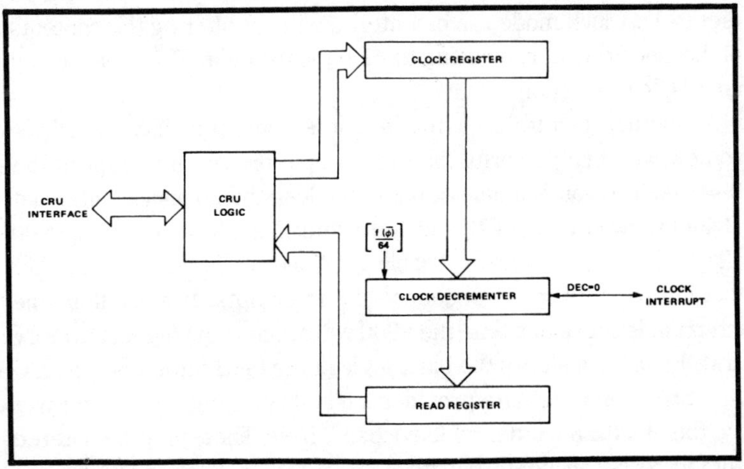

Fig. 3-3. Here is the real-time clock portion of the 9901 in block diagram form. Clock can be set or read via CRU interface, and produces interrupt when countdown reaches zero. (Courtesy of Texas Instruments)

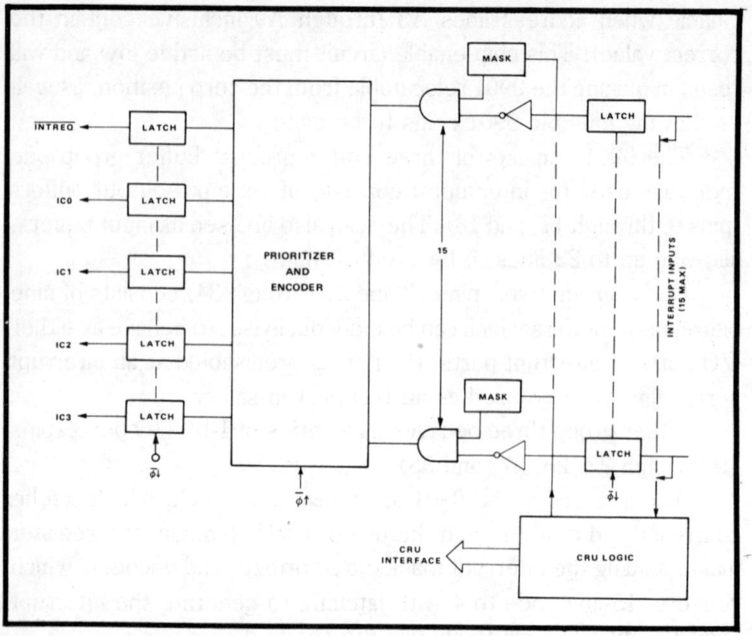

Fig. 3-4. This circuitry inside the 9901 chip converts up to 15 individual interrupt input lines into the 5-line code required by the 9900. (Courtesy of Texas Instruments)

rupts at controlled intervals, or as an event timer (the count is accessible). The clock can be set with an LDCR instruction, bit 0 on (set to 1). Clock mode can be entered without altering the contents of the clock register, by using the 1-bit instruction SB0, followed by an STCR instruction.

Another feature is a masked interrupt capability, which is somewhat more powerful than the simple priority interrupt of the 9900 itself. As an example, it might be desirable to disable interrupt 10 and allow interrupts 12 and 13 to remain enabled. With the 9900 alone, disabling 10 means disabling 12 and 13 as well. Remember that interrupt priorities sequence the interrupts. If more than one interrupt is active at a time the 9900 will process the highest priority first. Figure 3-4 shows the basic logic of the 9901 interrupt circuits.

Still another feature provides latched input-output lines for use by the 9900 and external devices. These lines may be altered without fear of an indeterminate state on output. Each line remains in its previous state until specifically changed. Figure 3-5 shows this 9901 feature. The line can be altered (if input) by an external device.

The importance of this unit lies in the fact that the CRU logic, including addressing, is already incorporated into the 9901. Note that 7 lines are dedicated to the I/O function and that a maximum of 16 lines may be so used.

TMS9902 ARCHITECTURE

The TMS9902 ACC device (Fig. 3-6) provides the ability to connect to the 9900 an asynchronous device, such as teletypewriters of any kind; ASCII compatible CRTs; keyboard-printer devices such as the TI Silent 700 series or any device using Start-Stop protocol, with a character length of 5 to 8 bits.

The 9902 will further generate any lateral parity option (even, odd, or none) and detect incorrect parity conditions. Even parity means the number of on bits is always kept even by turning an extra bit on and off. Odd parity means the number of bits is always kept odd. No parity means a parity bit is not added.

The transmit and receive rates are independently programmable from approximately 62 bits per second to approximately 76,000

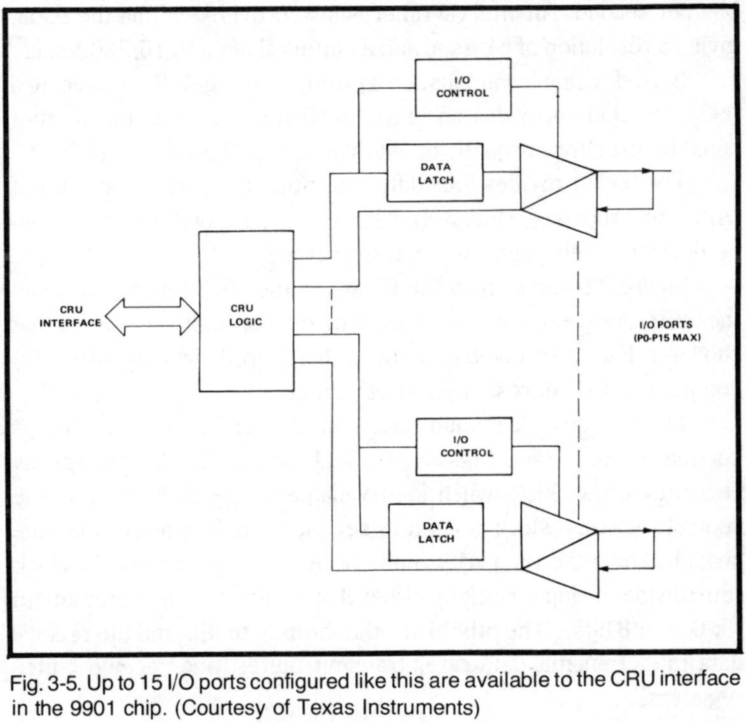

Fig. 3-5. Up to 15 I/O ports configured like this are available to the CRU interface in the 9901 chip. (Courtesy of Texas Instruments)

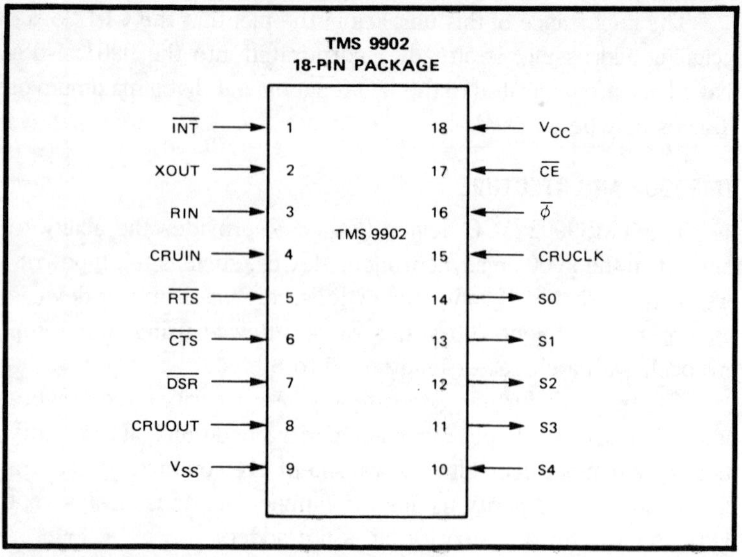

Fig. 3-6. Basing of the 18-pin TMS9902 package is shown here. Note that only 5 address lines are available. (Courtesy of Texas Instruments)

bits per second. An interval timer is also provided within the 9902, giving a resolution of 64 μsec and an interval of up to 16,320 μsec.

If used within a combination system (see Fig. 3-7) containing a 9901, the 9902 provides an extra interval timer. This extra timer could be used for purposes other than that of the one in the 9901.

The 9902 provides four different interrupts, which are output as one interrupt level (Fig. 3-8). The actual cause of the interrupt can be deciphered through the CRU interface.

Figure 3-9 shows how the 9900 and the 9902 (or the 9980 and the 9902) are connected together. The decode logic consists of that shown in Fig. 2-19 combined with a hardwired (or plug-alterable) comparator for address lines A3 through A9.

The two chips communicate over the CRU, using 32 bits as command words (see Figs. 3-10, 3-11, and 3-12). There are six registers in the 9902 which are available to the 9900. One is the control register, which is used to set the stop bit length (one, one and a half or two); the parity (none, even or odd); the master clock rate (divide the input clock by either 3 or 4); and the character length (5, 6, 7 or 8 bits). The others are the interval timer, and the receive data rate, transmit data rate, transmit buffer, and receive buffer registers.

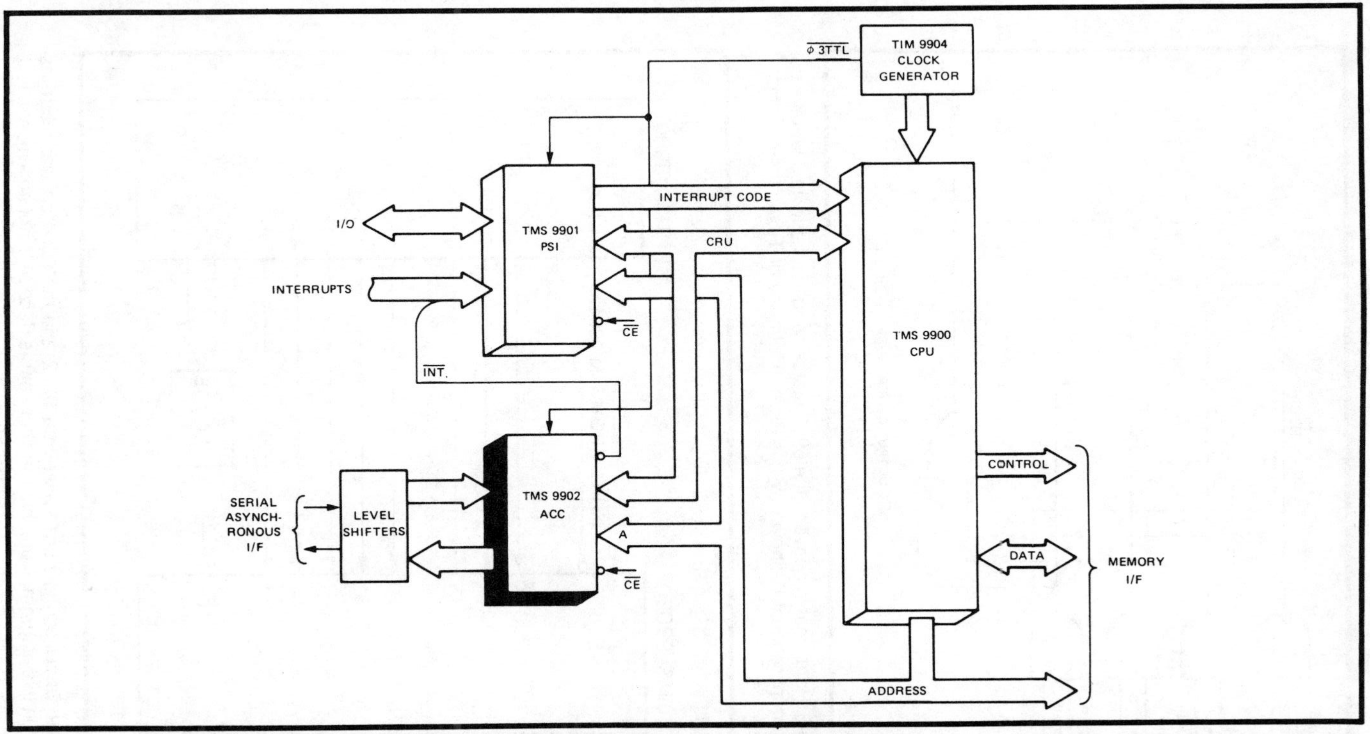

Fig. 3-7. Use of the TMS9902 in a 9900 system is shown here. The 9901 is not absolutely necessary, but simplifies the interrupt signalling greatly. (Courtesy of Texas Instruments)

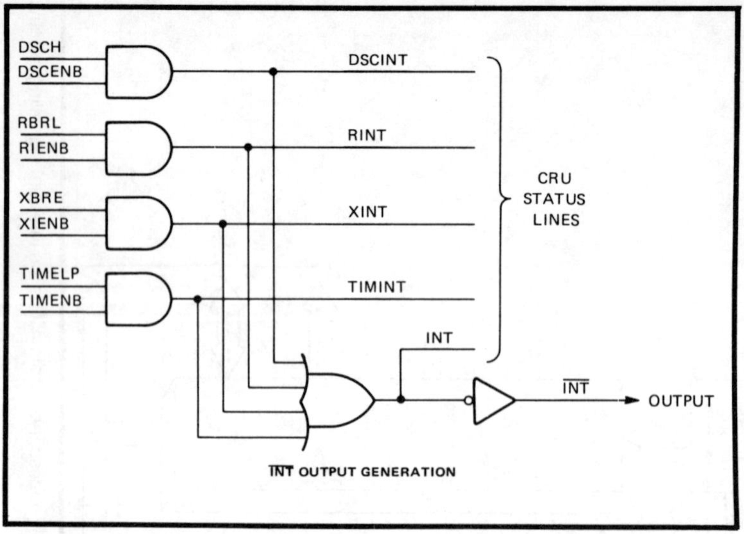

Fig. 3-8. Relationship between the 9902 status conditions and its generation of an interrupt request is shown by this logic. (Courtesy of Texas Instruments)

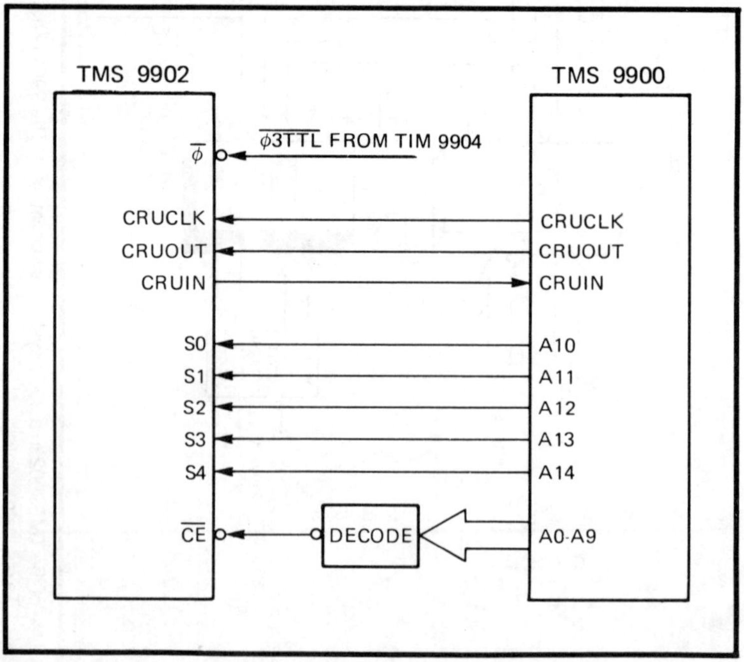

Fig. 3-9. Direct connections between a 9902 and the 9900 can be made as shown in this diagram. Note that the chip enable decode is not shown; see text for details. (Courtesy of Texas Instruments)

ADDRESS$_2$ S0 S1 S2 S3 S4	ADDRESS$_{10}$	NAME	DESCRIPTION
1 1 1 1 1	31	RESET	Reset device.
	30-22		Not used.
1 0 1 0 1	21	DSCENB	Data Set Status Change Interrupt Enable.
1 0 1 0 0	20	TIMENB	Timer Interrupt Enable
1 0 0 1 1	19	XBIENB	Transmitter Interrupt Enable
1 0 0 1 0	18	RIENB	Receiver Interrupt Enable
1 0 0 0 1	17	BRKON	Break On
1 0 0 0 0	16	RTSON	Request to Send On
0 1 1 1 1	15	TSTMD	Test Mode
0 1 1 1 0	14	LDCTRL	Load Control Register
0 1 1 0 1	13	LDIR	Load Interval Register
0 1 1 0 0	12	LRDR	Load Receiver Data Rate Register
0 1 0 1 1	11	LXDR	Load Transmit Data Rate Register
	10-0		Control, Interval, Receive Data Rate, Transmit Data Rate, and Transmit Buffer Registers

Fig. 3-10. Output bit address assignments for the 9902 are shown in this listing. Internal conditions for the chip are established by writing data to these bit addresses. (Courtesy of Texas Instruments)

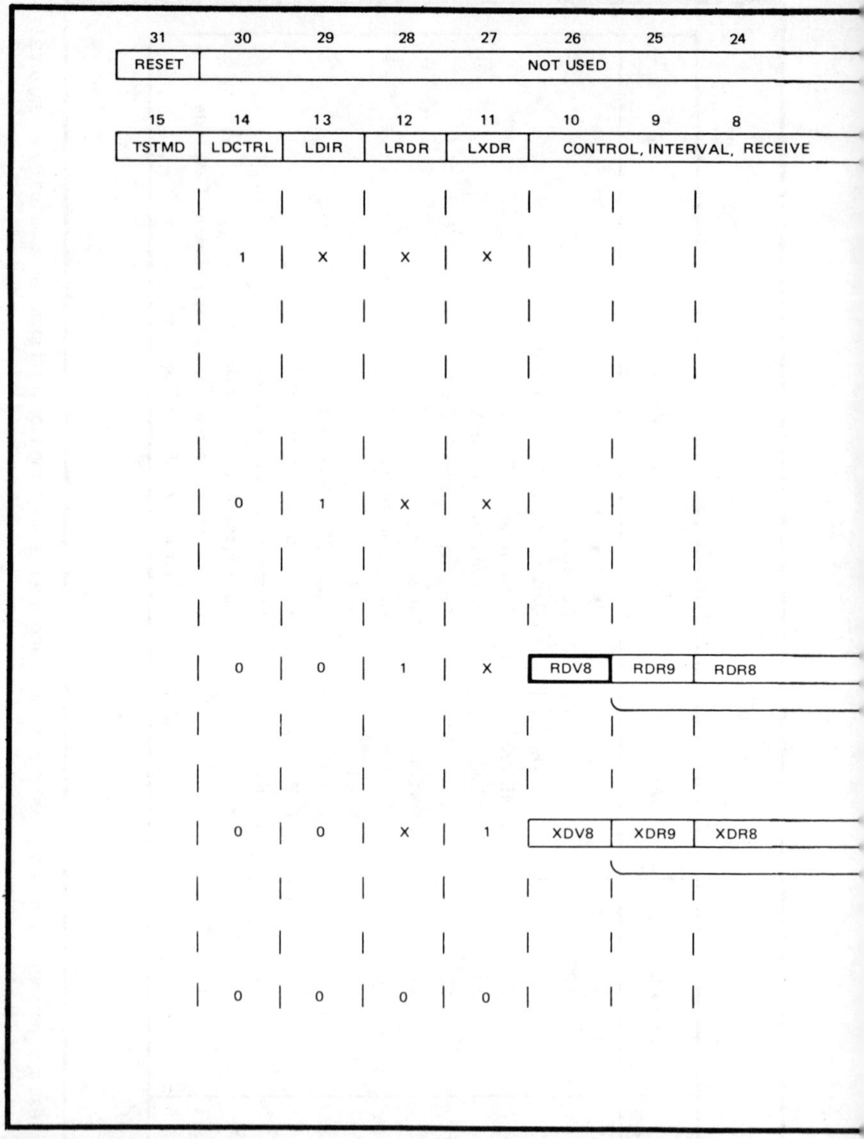

Fig. 3-11. This chart shows in greater detail how the 9902 is set up by writing to specific output bit addresses. The •STCR command is used to set bits into addresses 0 through 10, after appropriate values are written into addresses 14 through 11. (Courtesy of Texas Instruments)

Further data available to the 9900 (and the programmer) includes status flags and error flags. The 9902 interfaces to the outside world through TTL compatible circuits. There are times when an

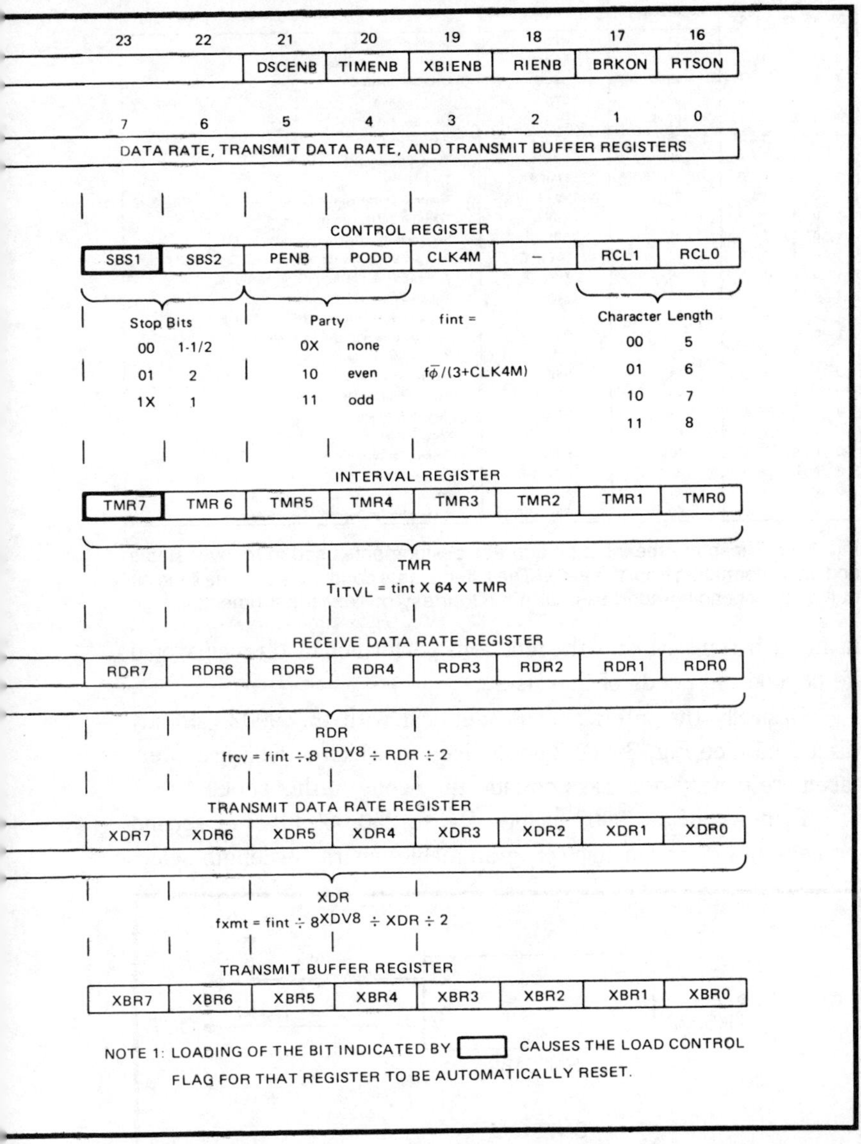

RS232 compatible interface is desired. This can be accomplished by the two circuits in Fig. 3-13.

TMS9903 SYNCHRONOUS COMMUNICATION CONTROLLER

Very little will be said about this integrated circuit, since it is rather doubtful that the typical user would be interested in actually

ADDRESS$_9$ S0 S1 S2 S3 S4	ADDRESS$_{10}$	NAME	DESCRIPTION
1 1 1 1 1	31	INT	Interrupt
1 1 1 1 0	30	FLAG	Register Load Control Flag Set
1 1 1 0 1	29	DSCH	Data Set Status Change
1 1 1 0 0	28	CTS	Clear to Send
1 1 0 1 1	27	DSR	Data Set Ready
1 1 0 1 0	26	RTS	Request to Send
1 1 0 0 1	25	TIMELP	Timer Elapsed
1 1 0 0 0	24	TIMERR	Timer Error
1 0 1 1 1	23	XSRE	Transmit Shift Register Empty
1 0 1 1 0	22	XBRE	Transmit Buffer Register Empty
1 0 1 0 1	21	RBRL	Receive Buffer Register Loaded
1 0 1 0 0	20	DSCINT	Data Set Status Charge Interrupt (DSCH • DSCENB)
1 0 0 1 1	19	TIMINT	Timer Interrupt (TIMELP • TIMENB)
1 0 0 1 0	18	—	Not used (always = 0)
1 0 0 0 1	17	XBINT	Transmitter Interrupt (XBRE • XBIENB)
1 0 0 0 0	16	RBINT	Receiver Interrupt (RBRL • RIENB)
0 1 1 1 1	15	RIN	Receive Input
0 1 1 1 0	14	RSBD	Receive Start Bit Detect
0 1 1 0 1	13	RFBD	Receive Full Bit Detect
0 1 1 0 0	12	RFER	Receive Framing Error
0 1 0 1 1	11	ROVER	Receive Overrun Error
0 1 0 1 0	10	RPER	Receive Parity Error
0 1 0 0 1	9	RCVERR	Receive Error
0 1 0 0 0	8	—	Not used (always = 0)
	7-0	RBR7-RBR0	Receive Buffer Register (Received Data)

Fig. 3-12. These are the input bit address assignments used to recover status and data information from the 9902. The listed status conditions are true if the bit at the corresponding address is a "1". (Courtesy of Texas Instruments)

using such a unit. Most of the functions performed by this chip would be beyond the needs of that user.

Basically the interfacing is identical with the 9902, already discussed (see Fig. 3-14). The devices to which a 9903 are interfaced are usually of a class outside the scope of this book.

Features of the 9903 include DC to 250,000 bits per second processing rates; dynamic (programmable) character length selec-

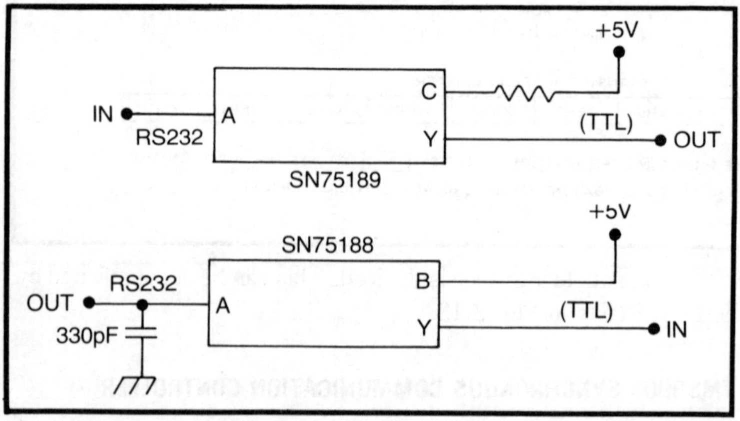

Fig. 3-13. These two circuits can be used to interface RS232 signal levels with the TTL signal levels of the 9902 chip.

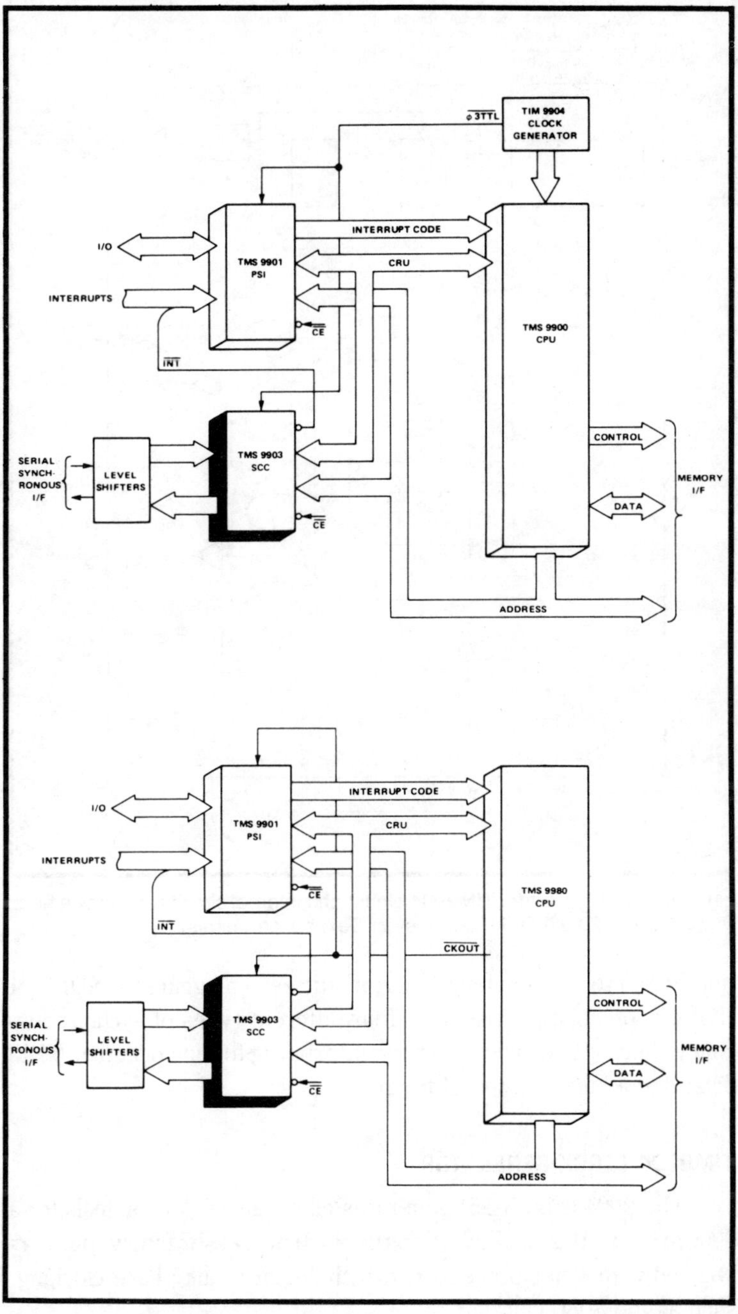

Fig. 3-14. The TMS9903 interfaces much like the 9902. (Courtesy of Texas Instruments)

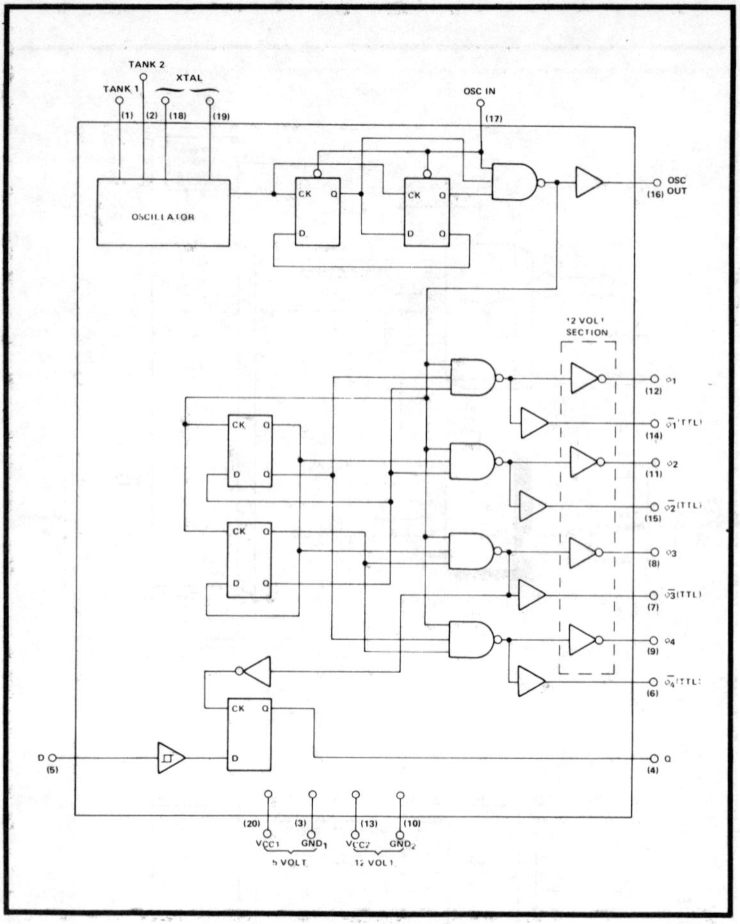

Fig. 3-15. Clock generator TIM9904 pinout and internal circuits are shown here. Device is in a 20-pin DIP. (Courtesy of Texas Instruments)

tion from 5 to 9 bits in length; automatic zero plugging for SDLC or HDLC protocols; provision for four different types of cyclic redundancy checks; two sync registers; interfacing for unclocked or NRZI data; and a built-in interval timer.

TIM9904 CLOCK GENERATOR

The 9904 (Fig. 3-15) generates all required clock signals for a 9900 system. It is not limited to the 9900 processor family, but may be used with other processors which require multiphase clocking, such as the 8080 chip family.

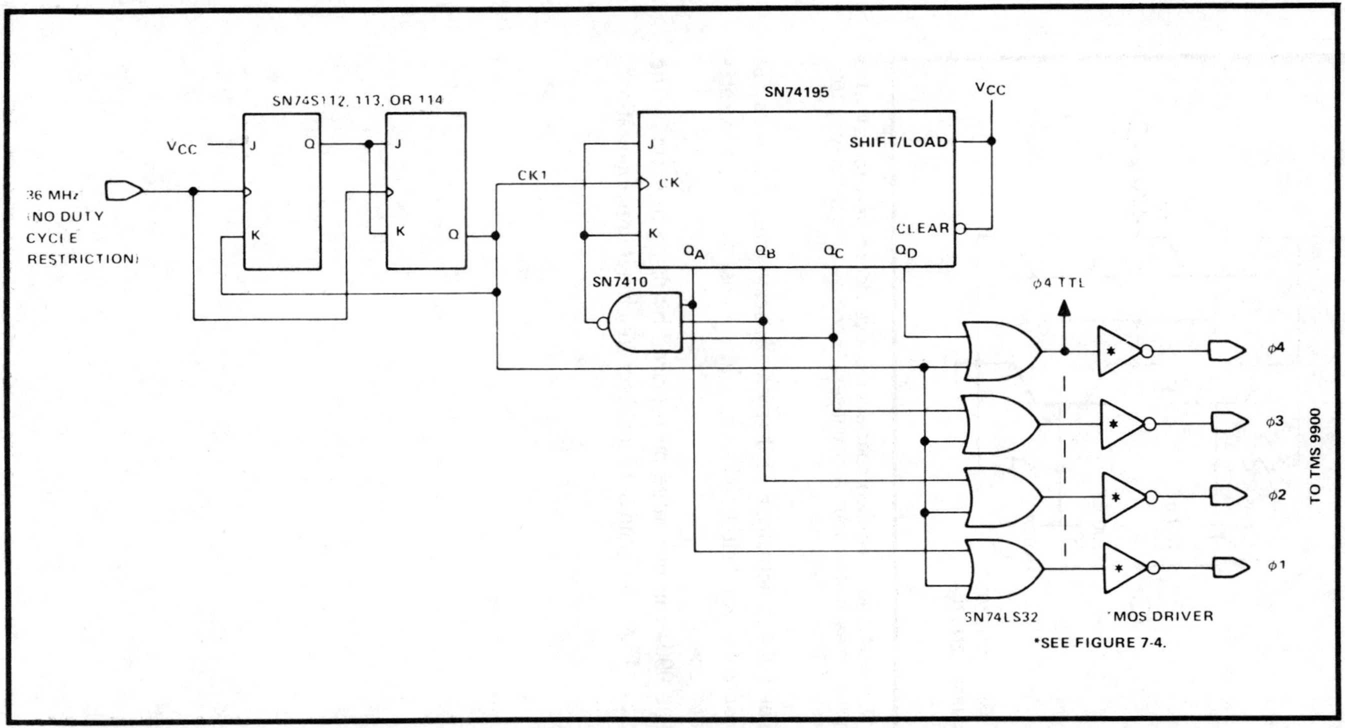

Fig. 3-16. Discrete logic can be used in this circuit to take the place of the 9904, but it costs more and does not perform so well. (Courtesy of Texas Instruments)

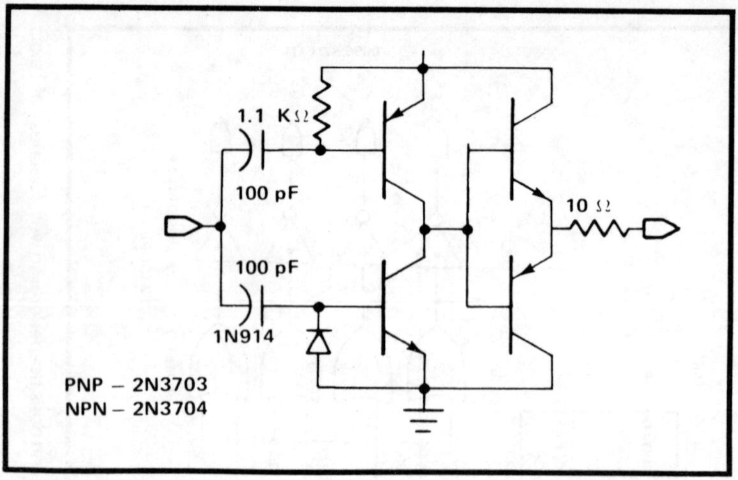

Fig. 3-17. If 9904 is not to be used, special MOS-level clock driver circuits like this are required on each of the four clock phases. All components can vary by 10%. (Courtesy of Texas Instruments)

The 9904 is actually a MSI (medium scale integration) circuit composed of several circuit blocks, at lower cost than the separate-unit total cost.

The 9904 can of course be replaced by discrete parts by the hardy. See Figs. 3-16 and 3-17 for discrete circuit implementation.

9900 System Design 4

The minimum 9900 system resembles the typical micro-processor evaluation system, usually expected of 8-bit processors. Figure 4-1 shows such a system, which contains the following;

256 words (512 bytes) of RAM;
1024 words of ROM or EPROM;
8 output lines, using CRUOUT;
8 input lines, using CRUIN;
a 4-phase clock, using the 9904;
one interrupt line (level 8);
a reset switch, to generate the RESET interrupt externally; and
an External Load signal to generate the LOAD interrupt.

Note that this entire system requires only 13 IC's, and 6 of these are memories. Besides the memories, the 9904, the 9900 itself, and the CRU devices (74LS151 and 74LS259) only three discrete logic chips are used. Two of these (the 74LS74's) generate the load pulse. The other provides inversion for three control signals (inverters A, B, and C). The simplicity of this design attests to the compatibility of the 9900 system circuits.

UPGRADING THE MINIMUM SYSTEM

Let us see how we can upgrade this minimal system:

A first step could be improving the CRU clocking system. A problem with the CRU interface shown is that the CRU clock signal

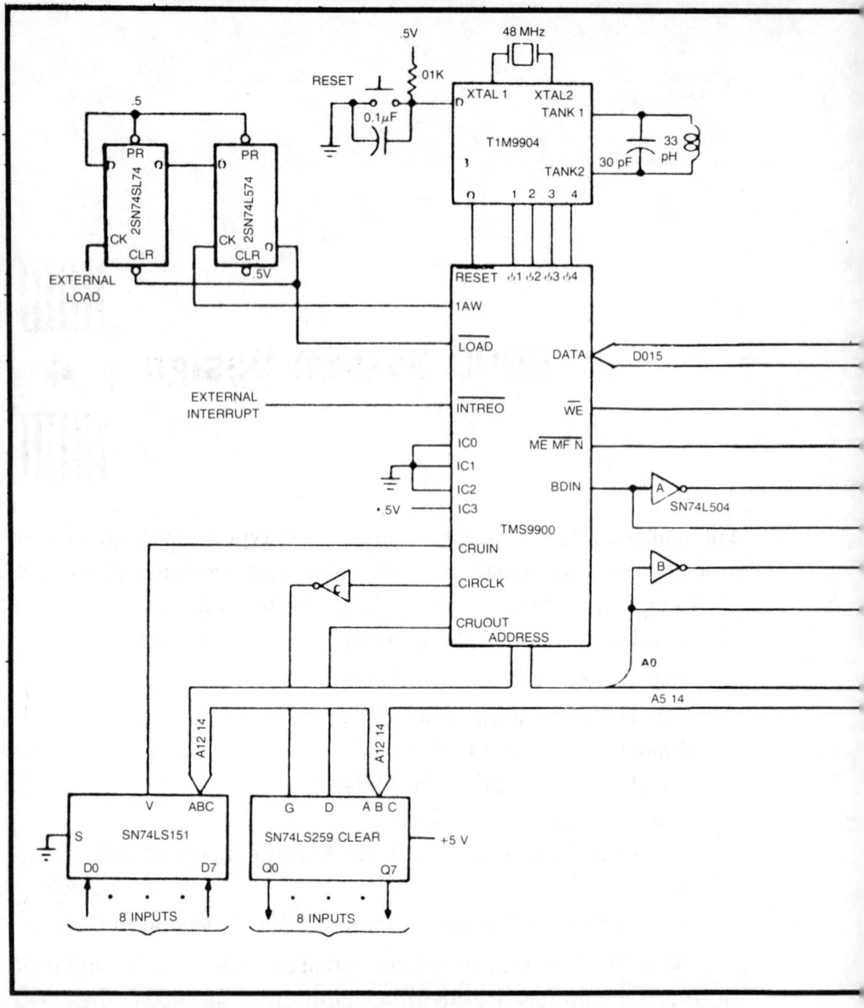

Fig. 4-1. A "minimum" system using the 9900 can be built by following this diagram. Refer to Fig. 2-3 for pin assignments of the 9900 and to Fig. 3-15 for pin assignments of the 9904. Basing of the memory chips and support logic can be obtained from TI data sheets available with the devices. Take special care to observe decoupling requirements on all power lines and prevent noise and crosstalk on signal lines. (Courtesy of Texas Instruments)

is also generated by the special instructions: IDLE; RESET; CKOF (CLOCK OFF); CKON (CLOCK ON); and LREX (LOAD OR RESTART EXECUTION). This could cause the CRU to operate incorrectly, so let us replace the inverter C by the circuit in Fig. 2-19. This gives us a properly decoded CRU clock, as well as decoded instructions.

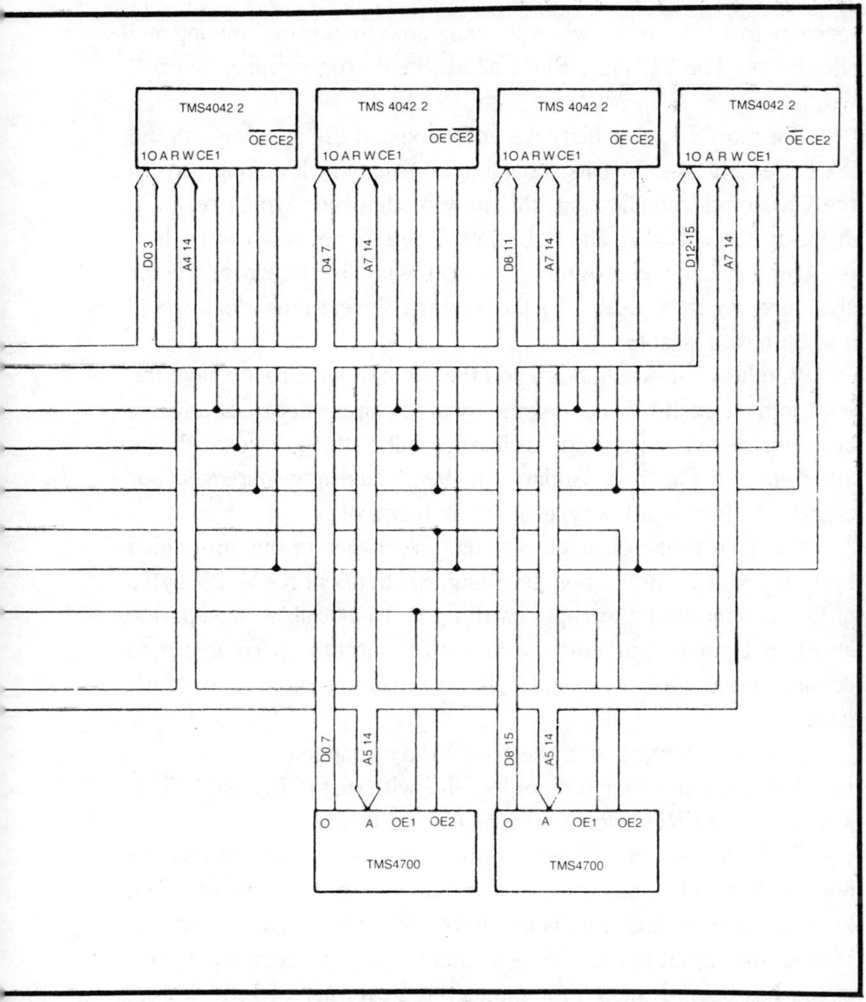

Another improvement would be expanding the RAM capacity. The limit of 256 words of RAM is obviously low for most uses; higher capacities might be desirable. The first choice, which requires the minimum change, is to replace the 4042-2 RAMS by 4047-45 RAMS and using address lines A5 and A6. An alternate choice, involving more chips, is to use the 4046-45 chips and address lines A3 through A6. The first choice gives a maximum of 1024 words, while the alternative gives 4096 words, or 8K bytes.

Similarly, we can expand the ROM capacity. Use of the 4908 EPROM will allow the user to expand the capacity of his read-only-memory to 1024 words, while allowing both field-programming and alterability. The 74S472 PROM allows field programming and 512 words.

For more I/O capability we could expand the system with the 9901. See Fig. 3-2 for basic coupling information. If combined with the CRU-clock modification, this new modification would result in dropping the 74LS151 and 74LS259. The I/O ports would replace the chips (including programmable ports). The interrupt vector structure would be usable by the system. A real-time-clock would also be now available.

Another step would be to add the 9902; if we already have the 9901 in the circuit, we need some form of chip select to distinguish between the two units. Address line A9 will do this job well with one inverter; see Fig. 4-2. Adding the 9902 has now increased our capacity to handle a teletype or other terminal.

What do these changes buy us? We have, in our up-graded system: external instruction decoding, 8K bytes of RAM, 2K bytes of ROM, 6 masked interrupts (with up to 15 available, as separate lines), 6 input/output ports with stable outputs to configure as needed, a real-time-clock, and a programmable asynchronous interface.

Let us now start with the heavy-duty changes:

First, replace the circuit of Fig. 4-2 with that of Fig. 2-12. This increases our CRU selection capacity to 8 devices.

Then, let us increase our storage capacity. Unfortunately, our poor 9900 was not meant to handle more than two standard TTL loads per line, so buffering is needed to boost the capacity further. We use the circuit in Fig. 4-3 as a sample buffering technique. This circuit has been designed for a maximum capacity of 1024 words. However the 74LS139 has 4 more selector lines available, so we can double the number of chip-selects. We can also boost capacity by using the same technique we used in our original explanation of the RAM. This gives us a total capacity, in RAM or ROM, of 32,768 words (or, if you wish, 65,536 bytes).

We can further subdivide any 4K word section into subsections, using our chip-select techniques.

Any section of our storage can contain ROM or EPROM.

With memory size increased, let us now expand our I/O capacity by adding a second 9902 to handle a serial device, such as a

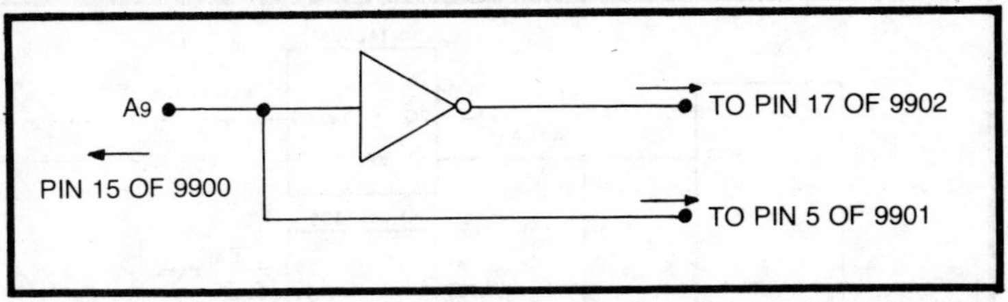

Fig. 4-2. This single-inverter circuit permits use of address line A9 to switch the chip-enable signal from a 9901 to a 9902 when your system includes one of each.

cassette drive. We can use one of our I/O ports from the 9901 as an on-off generator for the cassette deck.

We have now run into a terrible state of affairs. The ideal place for ROM or PROM is at the top of storage, but the reset function, which starts up the system, is in the wrong place (as far as vectors are concerned). Since the reset function is essential to clean start-ups, but the interrupt is not, let us perform a little trick on the system.

The load function should be activated as part of normal start-up anyway, so let us force it to be activated automatically. Figure 4-4 shows how to accomplish this feat. Because the LOAD signal will be on before the reset signal is finished, the vector at location 0 is not used and the one at FFFC (HEX) is used instead. ROM now becomes part of the upper storage.

If we like, we can add memory mapped I/O; this technique of I/O processing is particularly "sneaky" since it requires that an external device detect the signals used for memory access and simulate memory. Such devices are basically outside the scope of this book, since they require peripheral controllers.

We can also add DMA; this technique allows an external device to access memory while the 9900 goes off-line. The pins on the 9900 marked HOLD and HOLDA will allow this function to be performed. Figures 4-5 and 4-6 show a circuit (the Xs must be interconnected) which allows up to 16 devices to seize the memory bus on a priority basis, while Figs. 4-7 and 4-8 give an architectural view of this technique and a timing diagram. Since this technique is highly device dependent and, therefore, outside the scope of this book, we leave the rest to the reader.

As we saw earlier, DMA and memory mapped I/O are two techniques for getting data through the system without using the

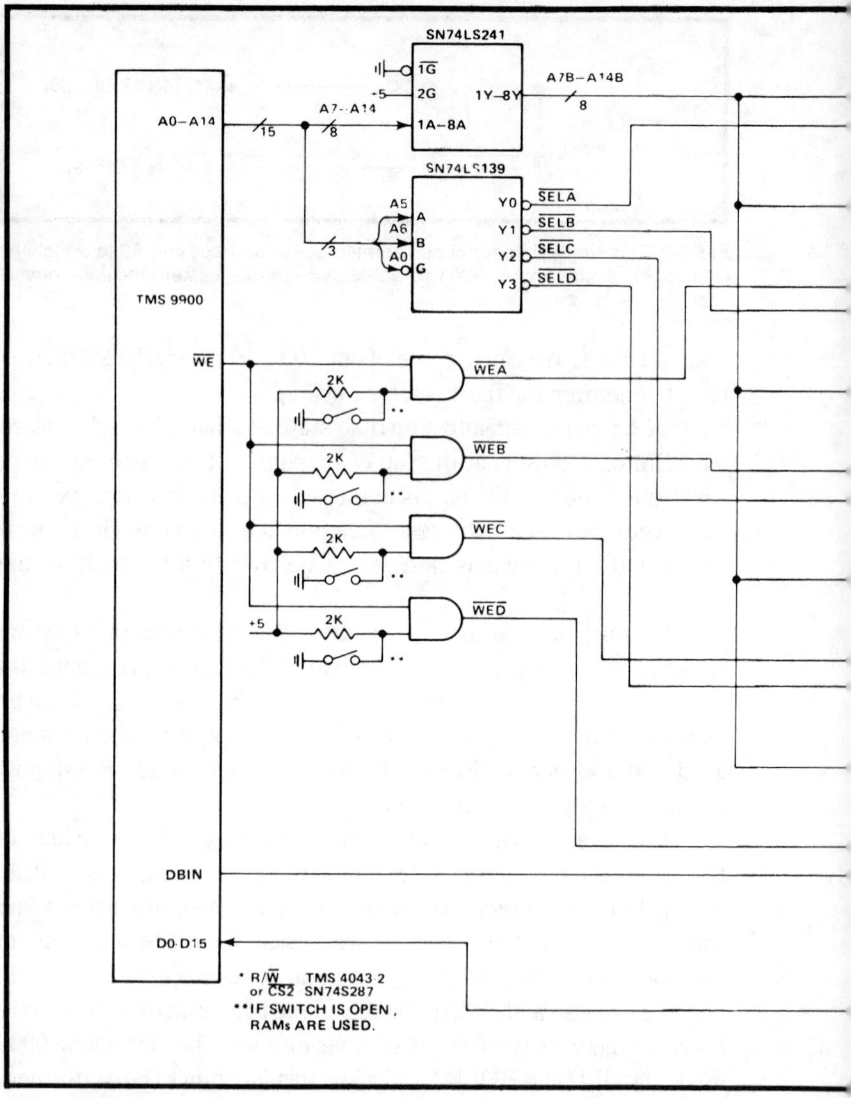

CRU. The DMA interfaces are very device dependent and outside the control of the 9900. The result is a problem. How do we get the data to the DMA device to allow it to perform its functions?

The answers are: via the CRU with interfacing, or via memory mapped I/O. We now see one of the main reasons for this form of I/O. Figure 4-9 is one such diagram of a simple 16 bit memory mapping interface.

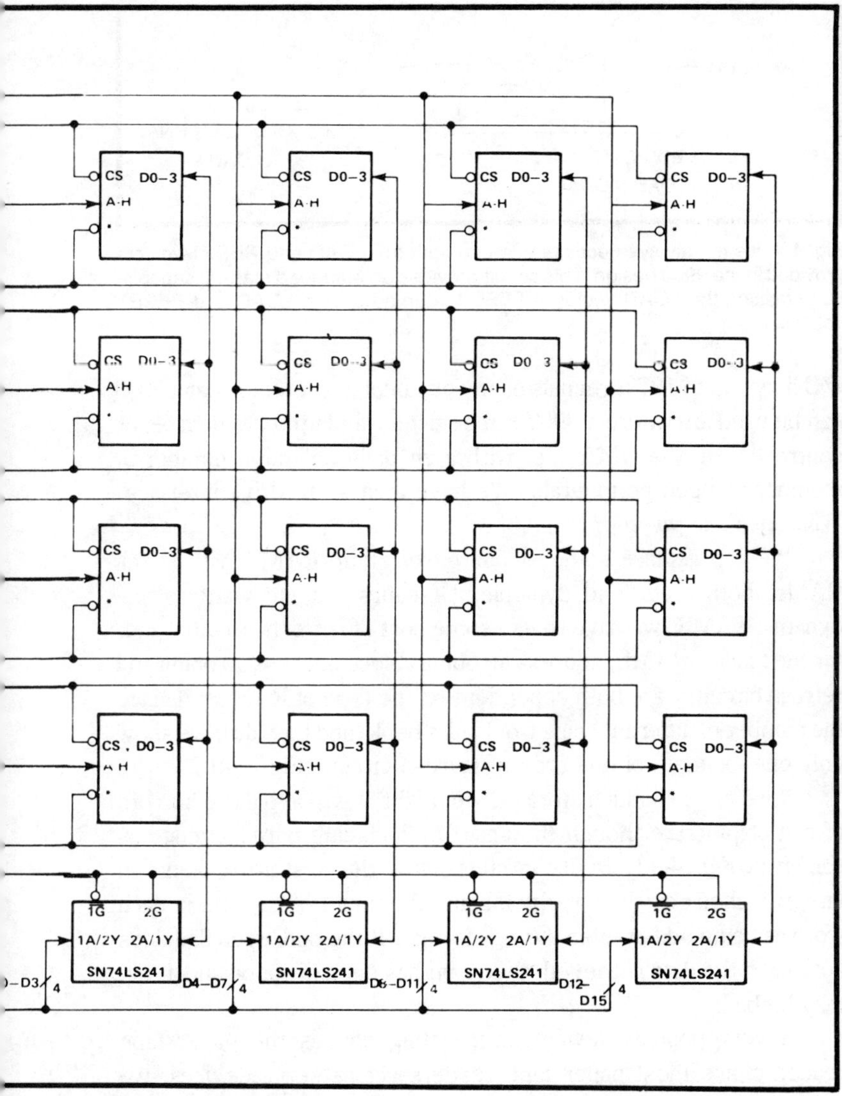

Fig. 4-3. When expanding the system to include additional memory, buffering and chip selection become essential. This circuit shows how to mix PROM and ROM chips. (Courtesy of TI)

WHAT HAVE WE GOT NOW?

Our system currently consists of: 32,768 words of mixed ROM and static RAM. We have a real time clock, vectored interrupts with masking, for up to 15 levels of interrupt, with at least 6 built in. We have 7 I/O lines, expandable (by sacrificing interrupt levels) to 16

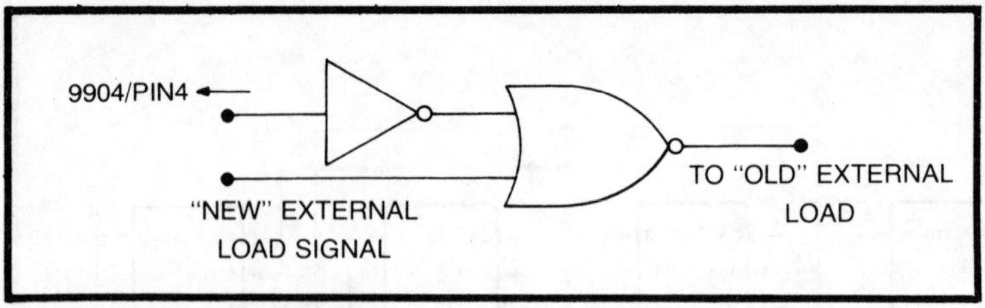

Fig. 4-4. It's not always necessary to use both the LOAD and RESET vectors provided in the 9900 design. This circuit provides an auto-load start-up capability, permitting the LOAD vector at FFFC to serve for both LOAD and RESET actions.

I/O lines; up to 127 terminals of any protocol (remember that a 9903 can be used anywhere a 9902 can be used); and up to 16 devices or controllers on the DMA line, with a virtually unlimited number of memory mapped peripherals. We have a cassette drive interface. What else can we add?

We can replace some of our bulky static RAMS with faster RAMs, both static and dynamic. Of course, if we want to use dynamic RAMS, we have to use some sort of refresh circuitry and, for the fancier RAMS, address strobing. Since address strobing and refresh circuitry are both dependent on the type of RAM, and since the number of different chips would fill a book (and they do), we show only one example of one type of refresh circuit (Fig. 4-10).

If we have so much storage, we might like to avoid the horrors of bad chips (rare though they are) by including parity circuits as shown in Fig. 4-11. Parity circuits allow the system to keep an integrity check on the data by logging the count of the bits in each word as being odd or even during storage. If the odd/even flag does not match the data retrieved, then a bit has been dropped and a chip may be bad.

A very popular device for inputting data is the paper tape reader. Since most paper tape readers act as serial devices, we could use a 9902 to interface to such a device. However, some readers have no serializing logic and simply input the data in parallel. Figure 4-12 shows one way to interface such a parallel device.

We may wish to mix slow memory with fast, in order to improve the cost-effectiveness of our system. This requires that the 9900, which has to know that the memory is valid, be signaled somehow. Figures 4-13 and 4-14 show how this can be done; Fig. 4-15 shows the timing requirements.

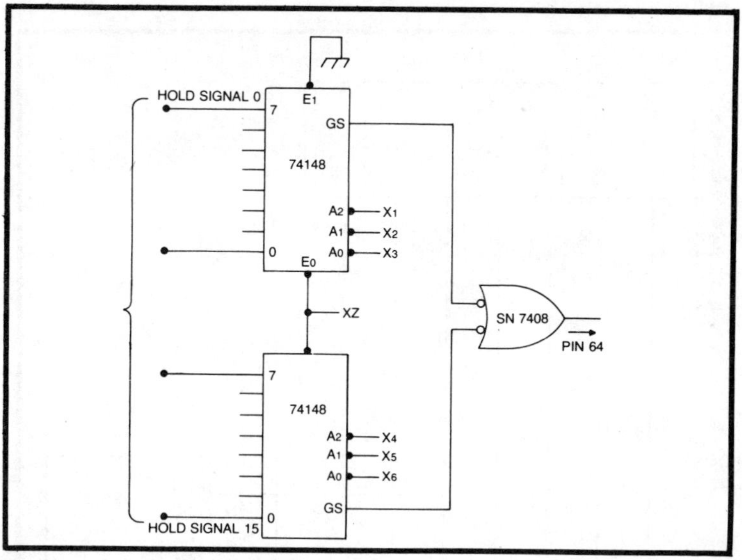

Fig. 4-5. For direct memory access applications we must be able to recognize requests to HOLD the 9900 off of the bus lines. This circuit prioritizes up to 16 different HOLD requests.

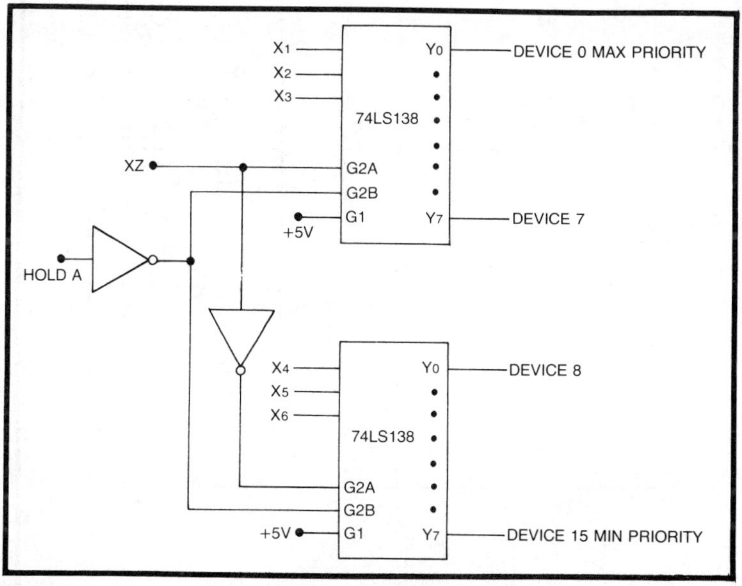

Fig. 4-6. No DMA activity can be permitted until the HOLD request is acknowledged. This circuit provides prioritized HOLD acknowledgement, for use with the circuit of Fig. 4-5. Together the two circuits permit up to 16 different DMA activities in conjunction with normal processing.

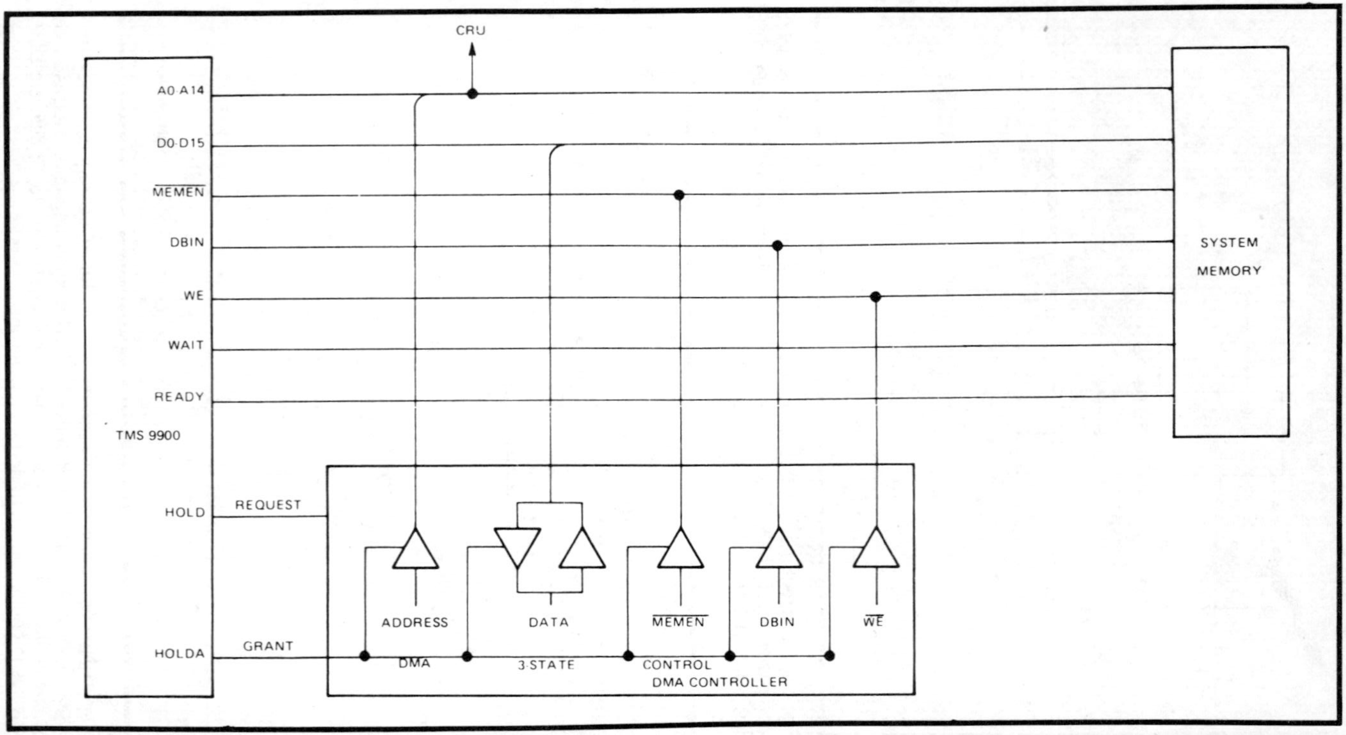

Fig. 4-7. For DMA applications, each DMA controller must have access to the system memory just as does the 9900. This block diagram summarizes bus control requirements for a single DMA controller. (Courtesy of Texas Instruments)

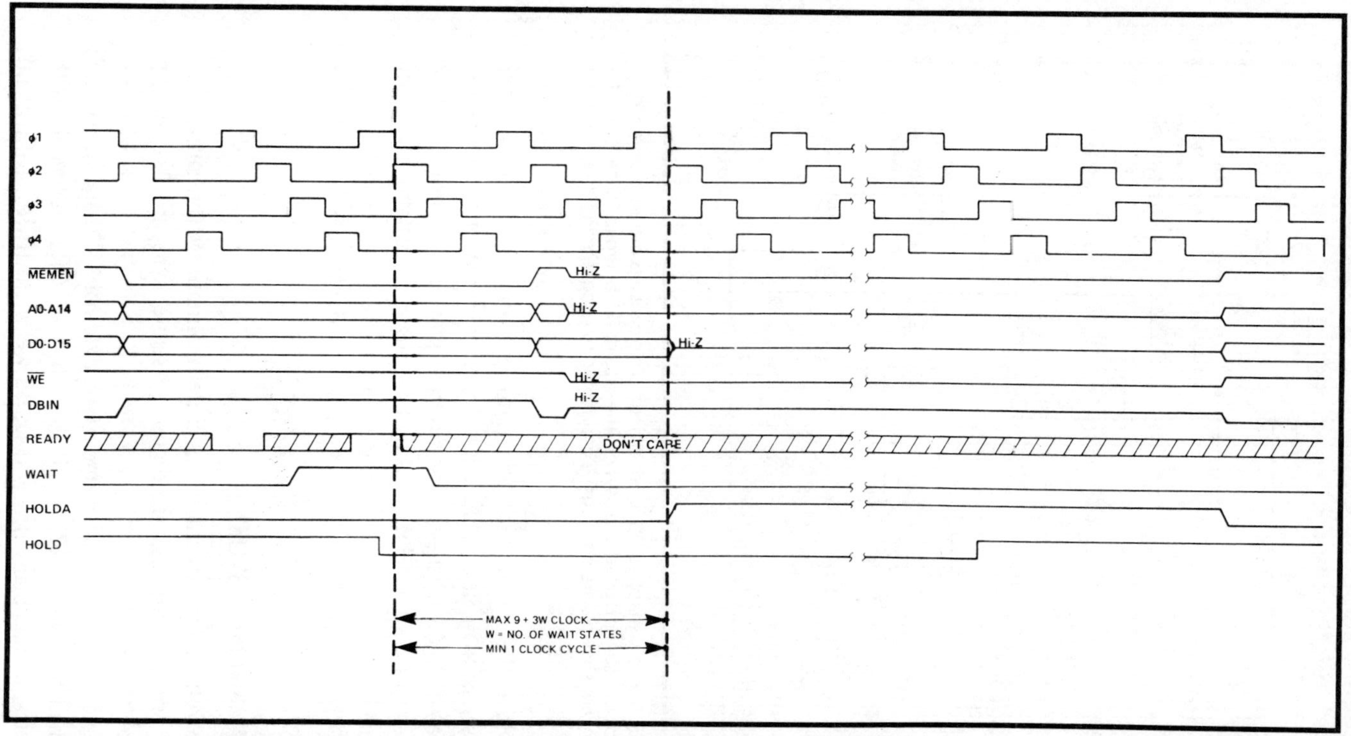

Fig. 4-8. Design of a DMA controller requires careful attention to system timing. All essential signals are shown here in relation to the four system clock signals. (Courtesy of Texas Instruments)

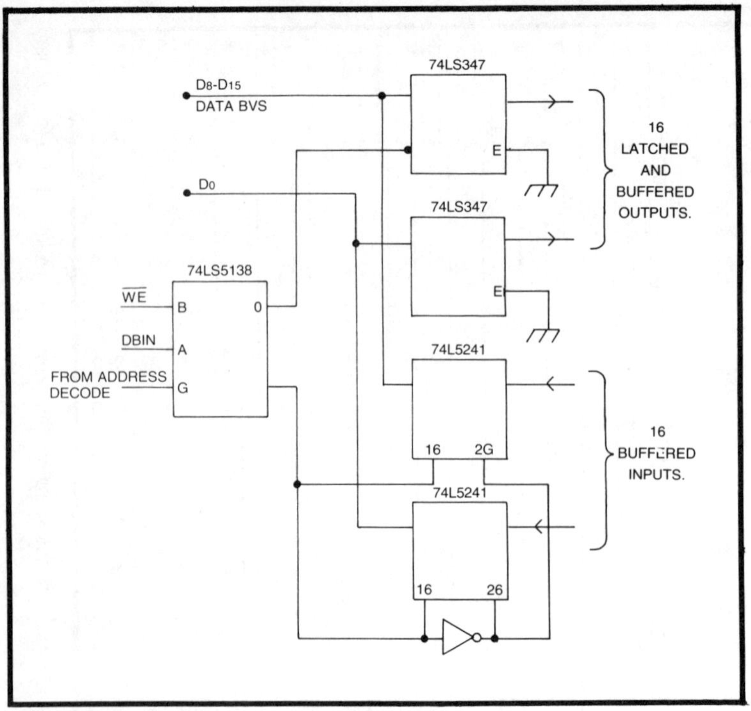

Fig. 4-9. Memory-mapped I/O is not difficult. This circuit provides a single 16-bit word of memory-mapped I/O. When the assigned address is decoded (by circuitry not shown), the data bus is connected to either the input or the output port.

Have we taken this "minimum" system as far as we can? Almost, since most of what is left depends on external constraints. We can still add mass-storage devices; plotters and other graphic devices; printers, card readers and punches; or just about anything we could think of. However, none of these devices are really part of the 9900. They are, rather, peripherals and don't really belong in this book.

THE MAXIMUM SYSTEM?

We have by now taken our little minimum system pretty far. Have we reached the maximum possible system? Not in the slightest.

Our system can easily handle 64K bytes of ROM and RAM, can communicate with 127 terminals, can use CRT terminals with graphics, and as many floppy discs as we wish. If we have big and

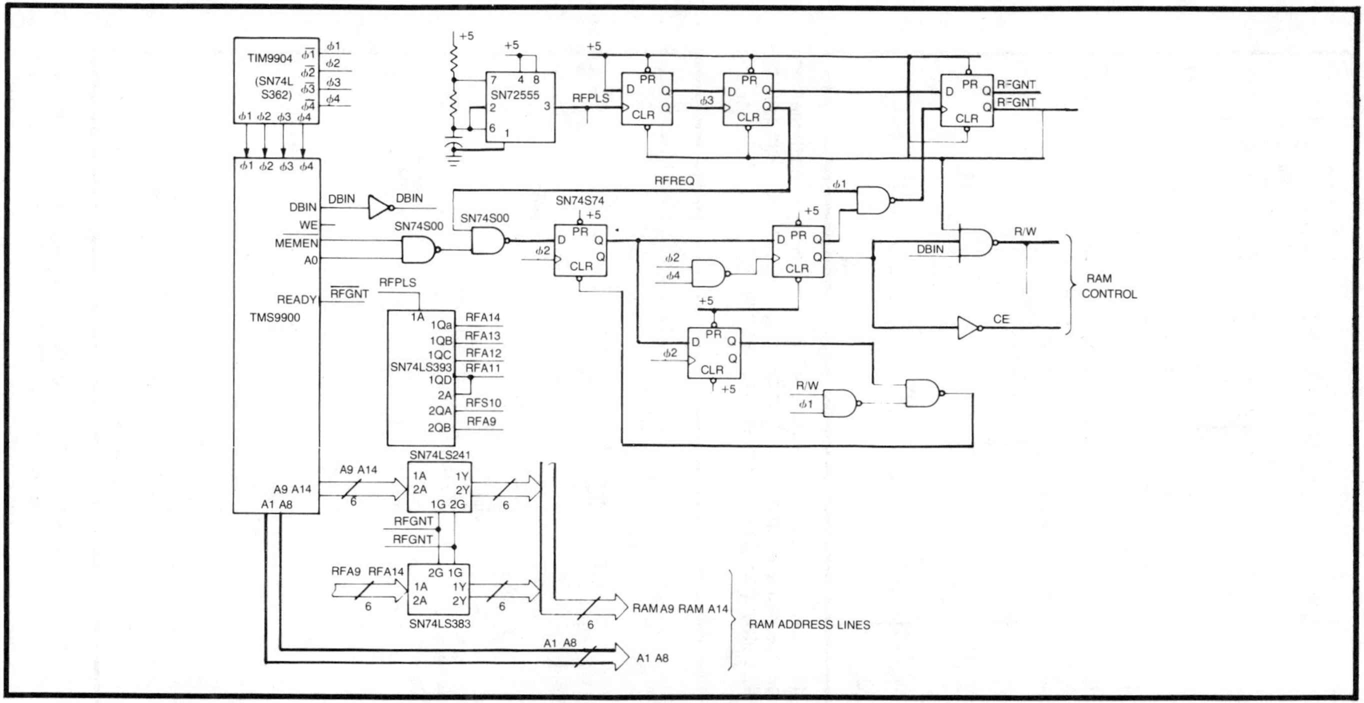

Fig. 4-10. Dynamic RAM is less costly than static ram, both in terms of component cost and power consumption, but requires special refresh circuitry to keep data valid. This circuit demonstrates "cycle-stealing" refresh action for such dynamic RAM devices as the 4051. (Courtesy of Texas Instruments)

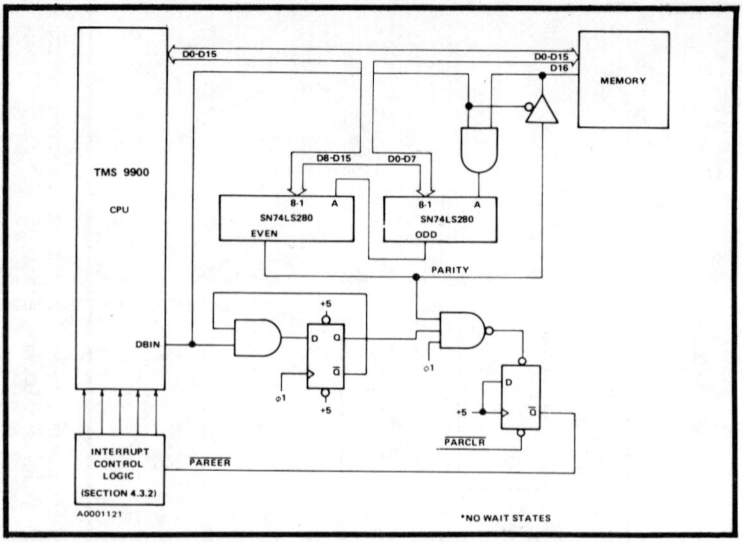

Fig. 4-11. For better confidence in system reliability the parity of each memory word can be checked at each access. This circuit generates and checks parity, with no wait states. (Courtesy of Texas Instruments)

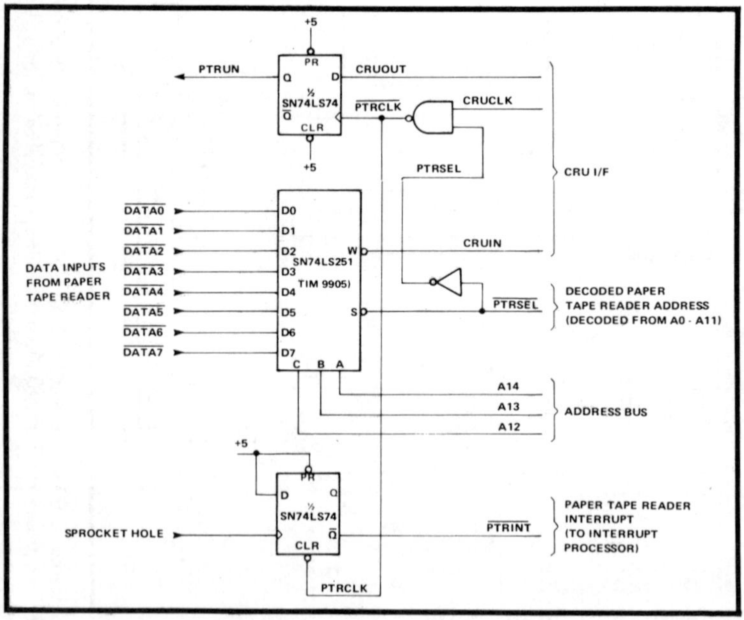

Fig. 4-12. Specific peripheral devices require specific interfaces. This circuit, to connect an 8-level paper tape reader, is typical of such device-dependent designs. (Courtesy of Texas Instruments)

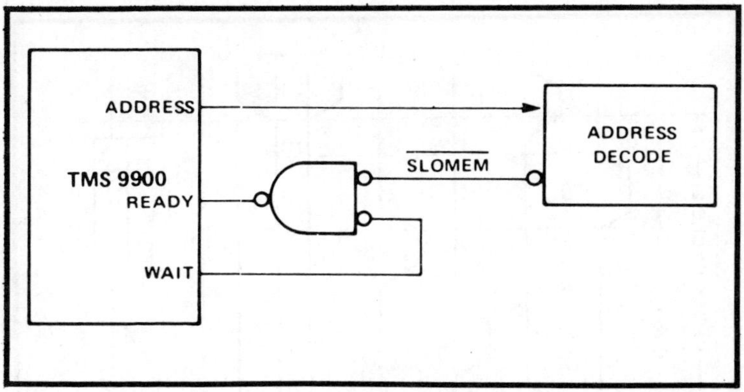

Fig. 4-13. If slow memory is to be used, "wait" states must be introduced into normal processor action to give the memory time to respond. This circuit provides one wait state on each memory access. (Courtesy of Texas Instruments)

grand ideas it can handle cartridge (and bigger) discs. We can interface with printers, card readers and plotters. And, if we wish, we can communicate with other computers in a network.

We could even design multi-processor configurations, with memory mapping and banking (techniques to expand our storage capacity). We could use many different output devices for our 9900 system. The only limits are our ambition, time, and money.

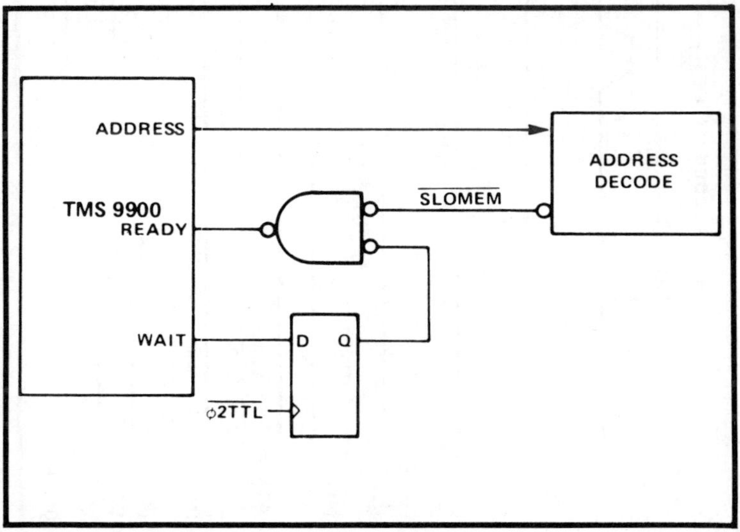

Fig. 4-14. For even slower memory, two wait states may be necessary. This circuit provides them. (Courtesy of Texas Instruments)

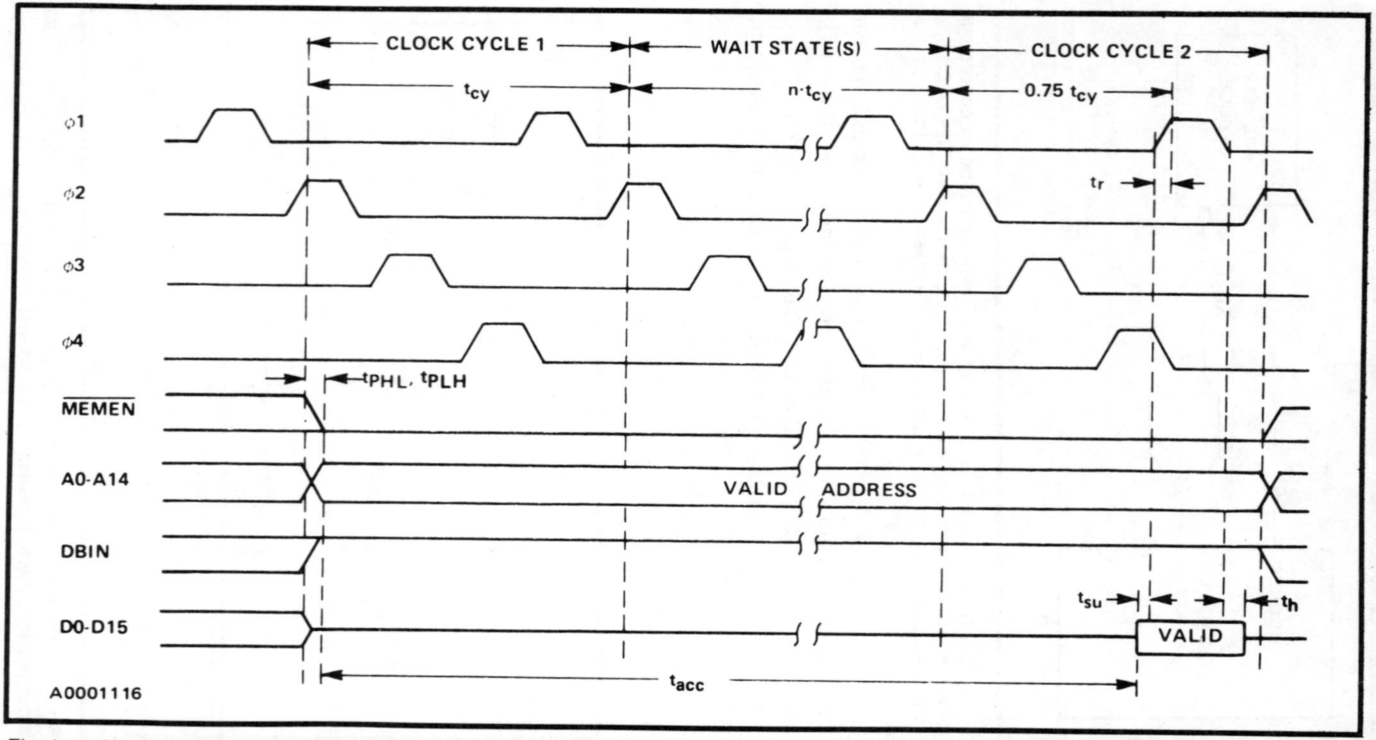

Fig. 4-15. All memory access calculations require accurate knowledge of system timing. All essential signals are shown here, referenced to the time of one cycle of the 9900 clock frequency (that is, 0.333 us for a 3-MHz clock). (Courtesy of Texas Instruments)

5 Hints About Peripherals

Many hobbyists prefer to have, instead of a printer, a CRT interface to handle the printout from their systems. The reasons are quite simple. The electronics in a CRT terminal are far less expensive than the mechanical parts in a printer. The electronics of a CRT system are already packaged into every TV set sold. The speed of a CRT based system will easily beat any hard-copy terminal.

There are of course many ways to interface a CRT to the 9900 system we have developed. We may use a separate terminal, such as the Lear-Seigler ADM series or any other terminal of ASCII RS232C or 20 mA loop type. There are many terminals of this class, usually known as "Teletype replacement" CRT terminals. Other examples include the VUCOM terminals and the TI VDT913 (see Fig. 5-49). These can all be interfaced through a 9902. The terminals that are known as CRT-specific terminals, such as the IBM 3270 series, the VUCOM 2 terminals and the IBM 2260 series, are meant to be seen by the processor as a CRT and not as any sort of replacement. These usually are connected through a 9903 (SCC) device.

The CRT interface is described here in general terms only, since a full set of plans would require a book by itself.

Figure 5-1 shows a basic block diagram of such a system interface, while Fig. 5-2 shows a block diagram of the display controller.

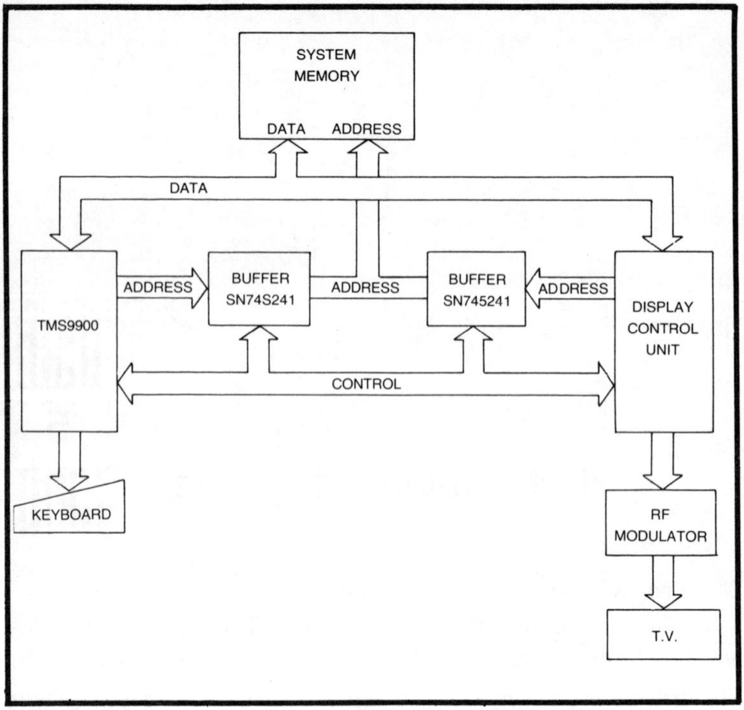

Fig. 5-1. Design of a video I/O system requires detailed knowledge of both video and digital signal requirements. This block diagram can serve as a starting point for design of a system using shared memory. Both the 9900 and the display control unit have access to the common system memory.

We can see a problem with this technique since the display controller needs to access storage quite often. Two approaches are possible: We can use DMA logic to interface both devices to storage. The 74S241 tri-state BUFFER chip can allow us to create such a system, see Fig. 5-3 for an example. We can, alternatively, use a different technique with a special memory block set up in an unusual fashion, which cycle-steals time from the 9900 (see Fig. 5-4).

This memory block would contain buffer latches such as the 74LS374 and the 74LS241 chips, issuing a WAIT to the 9900 if it is servicing the display controller when a request for a word in the block becomes available. Should you wish to build a system using a display controller in either fashion above, a strong grounding in digital electronics and TV signal generation is recommended. The following chips should be investigated: The 74S412 makes nice data buffers, the TMS3409 recirculating shift registers, the 74LS253 for character and graphics control, the 74S472 as a character generator PROM and control signal PROM, and the 74LS241 for DMA control buffers. We can go no further on this subject within this book.

DISC SYSTEMS

The term "floppy disc" was coined by some rather annoyed people when they first saw an IBM "diskette." The diskette was designed to hold the "microcode" for an IBM 370/145 computer. Because it resembled a magnetic disc (which it was) and was flexible enough to "flop" when waved around, someone called it a "blasted FLOPPY disc." He (or she) was only half-right.

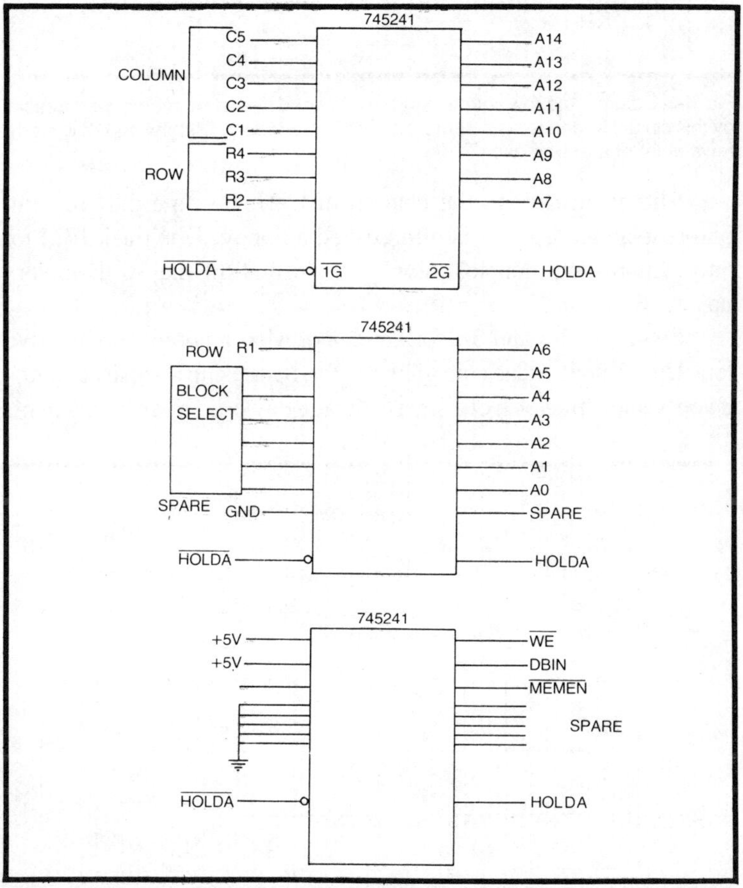

Fig. 5-2. Essential elements of a display controller include counters to keep track of rows and columns, a character generator, and blanking generator. Control circuitry must develop video sync pulses at appropriate intervals.

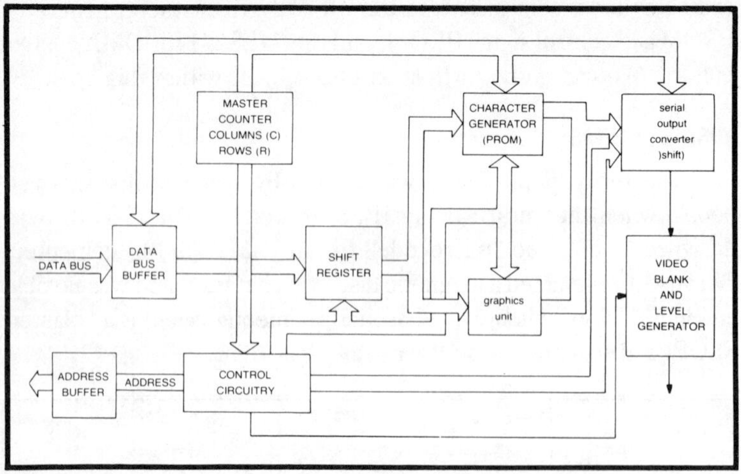

Fig. 5-3. Column and row counts can be converted to system memory addresses by this circuit, intended as a sample of DMA interfacing. Display capability is 16 rows of 64 characters each.

The name has, to the chagrin of IBM, become part of computerese and a diskette is often called a floppy. Don't ask IBM for information about floppies, however, since it still makes them very upset.

See Figs. 5-5 and 5-6 for an idea of what a floppy and its drive look like. A floppy disc controller can be built using a separate 9900, if you wish, in the form of a smart storage device. Texas Instruments

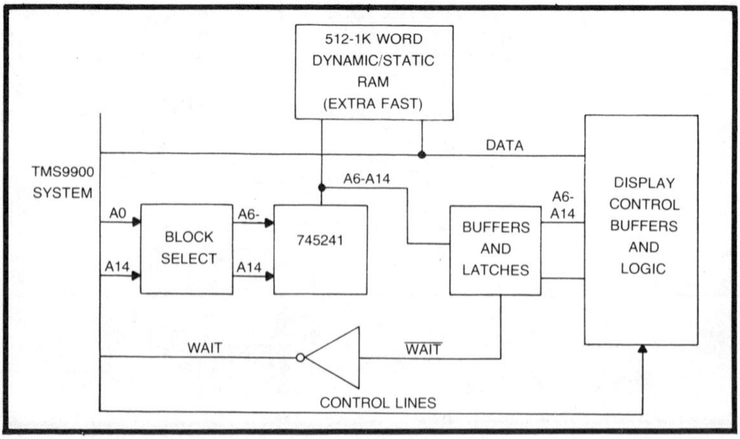

Fig. 5-4. Cycle stealing can be used instead of DMA to interface the display controller to memory. This diagram shows how.

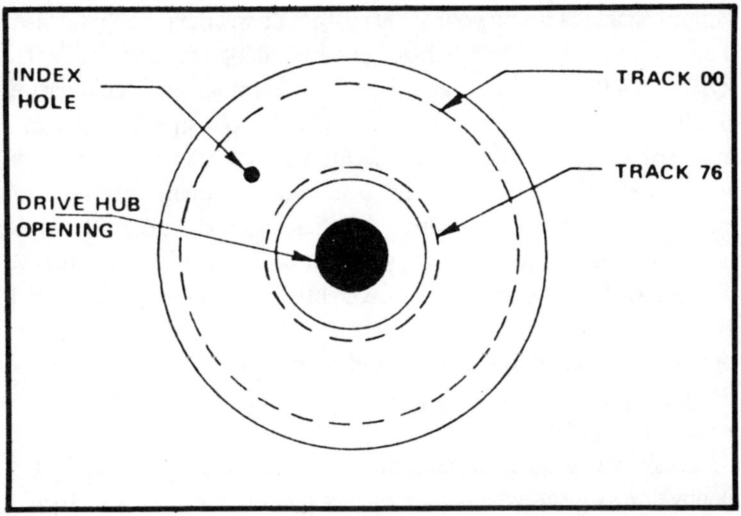

Fig. 5-5. Floppy disk layout looks like this. Disk itself is enclosed in protective envelope and should never be removed from it. Total of 77 tracks are available for storage of data.

has, in fact, developed such a design as an example of the sheer flexibility and power of their 9900 processor, but I personally believe that this is pure over-kill. You may find a floppy or series of floppies very useful, but there are several ways to obtain them already to run. Any computer mag will have information on available units from various manufacturers. These manufacturers will either have a

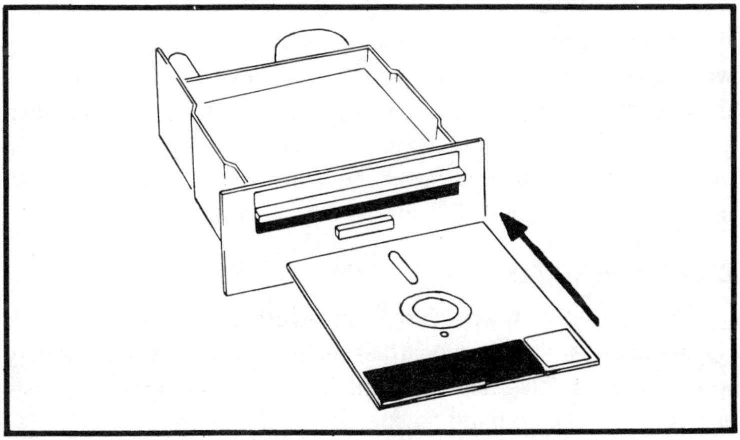

Fig. 5-6. Typical floppy disk drive unit has slot with hinged lid. When disk (in envelope) is inserted in slot and lid is closed, stored data is available for reading.

floppy capable of fitting your 9900 system or will devise an interface. Texas Instruments already has a pre-built floppy for use with a 990 system, all 9900 systems and their TTL versions are called part of the 990 series machines. Of course you can obtain a floppy with a standard interface and modify it to fit. You will have to make these basic modifications most likely; a memory mapping interface for control and status. If the floppy delivers bytes and generates byte address, then you will need byte/word buffering for both data and addresses. If you wish to use a CRU interface for control lines then reread the section on CRU interfacing. Because of the variety of options available at any stage of designing such a system, we must leave this up to you to design. Once again, this project is outside the scope of this book.

Should you wish to have more capacity than is available in a floppy disc system, with higher access speeds, you may wish to look at cartridge discs, such as the Texas Instruments DS31.

If even cartridge discs are insufficient, you may wish to look at even higher capacity systems. These are, usually, of the 2314-compatible, 3330-compatible or "Winchester technology" drives, with single drive capacities of:

- 2311 type drives, to 7.25 megabytes
- 2314 type drives, to 29.0 megabytes
- 3330 type drives, to 200 megabytes
- 3340 (Winchester), to 70 megabytes
- 3350 (Winchester), to 300 megabytes.

If you need such capacities, you should remember the price rises with capacity and speed, though you do get more for your dollar as the price rises. Interfacing becomes much more tricky and complex. Devices of this caliber take up more space. Devices like this use up more power. This book is about the hobbyist and home computer, not your own versions of Colossus (and Guardian?).

OTHER PERIPHERALS

Plotters are now available, from several manufacturers, which can interface through a standard asynchronous interface, as if they were teletypes. This can allow you do your own graphs, drawings and other plotter oriented functions.

Unless you wish to use these devices seriously, be warned that they are still expensive in more ways than one. As an example, that card reader might not be too expensive to purchase, but you will also need a keypunch....

You may also wish to add a line printer. These printers are far faster than the typical 10 to 40 characters per second printers used by the hobbyists. These printers can reach speeds of up to 2000 lines per minute (yes, two thousand), with up to 132 characters per line. The equivalent speed in characters per second is around 4,000 CPS. Once again, you can choose from several interface options. You can use the CRU to output bytes and control. A 16-bit interface should be adequate. You can use an ACC interface such as the 9902. Of course you can always use memory mapped I/O, or perhaps you would prefer to use the DMA and send full lines at a time, with a buffer.

Should you wish you can add a card reader to read your programs and data. When combined with a printer and some control card capabilities in your software, a card reader will give you a batch system, allowing unattended operation.

By using a 9903 SCC and a data-link you can hook up your system to a larger computer, as if you had a "Remote Job Entry" (RJE) system. Since there is nothing stopping you from making the other computer another 9900 based system, you can start building your own network.

We can use time-sharing to allow our friends access to the machine. We might even charge for the time and resources (shades of the service bureau).

Basically the 9900, like any well-designed computer, is limited more by the ingenuity of the users and designers than anything else. We have gone as far as we can in this book. The rest is up to you!

Appendix Instruction Codes

This appendix contains the instruction codes of the 9900, the 990/4 and the 990/10. As you will quickly see, the instruction set of these computers has been carefully thought out to allow efficient implementation on both an LSI microprocessor and a TTL minicomputer.

You will also see why it is easy to fall in love with the 9900 family. Just compare this instruction set with that of any other microprocessor.

TMS 9900 INSTRUCTION SET

A. 1 DEFINITION

Each TMS 9900 instruction performs one of the following operations:

- Arithmetic, logical, comparison, or manipulation operations on data
- Loading or storage of internal registers (program counter, workspace pointer, or status)
- Data transfer between memory and external devices via the CRU
- Control functions.

A.2 ADDRESSING MODES

TMS 9900 instructions contain a variety of available modes for addressing random-memory data (e.g., program parameters and flags), or formatted memory data (character strings, data lists, etc.). The following figures graphically describe the derivation of the effective address for each addressing mode. The applicability of addressing modes to particular instructions is described in Section 3.5 along with the description of the operations performed by the instruction. The symbols following the names of the addressing modes [R, *R, *R+, @ LABEL, or @ TABLE (R)] are the general forms used by TMS 9900 assemblers to select the addressing mode for register R.

A.2.1 WORKSPACE REGISTER ADDRESSING R

Workspace Register R contains the operand.

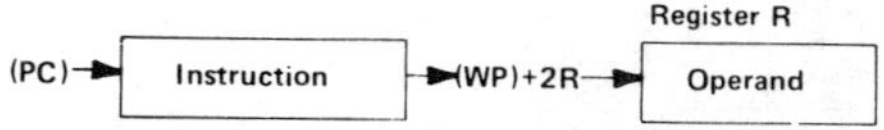

A.2.2 WORKSPACE REGISTER INDIRECT ADDRESSING * R

Workspace Register R contains the address of the operand.

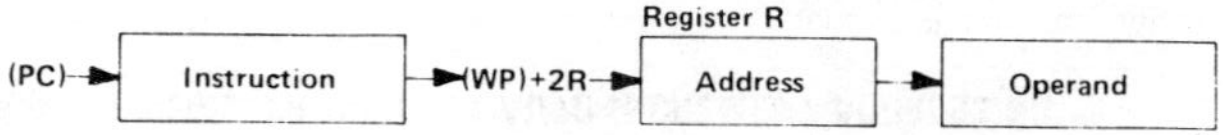

A.2.3 WORKSPACE REGISTER INDIRECT AUTO INCREMENT ADDRESSING *R+

Workspace Register R contains the address of the operand. After acquiring the operand, the contents of workspace register R are incremented.

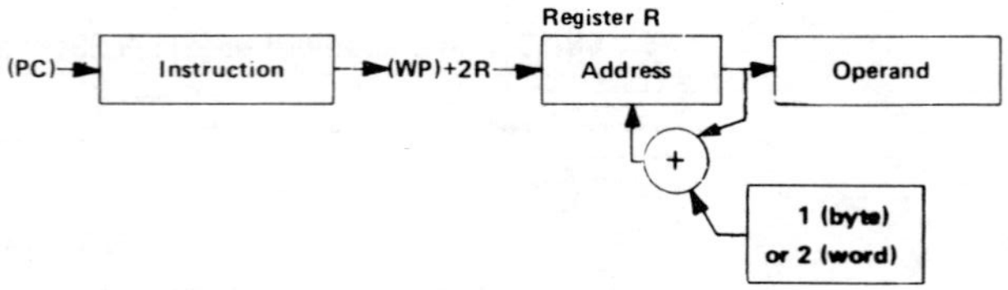

A.2.4 SYMBOLIC (DIRECT) ADDRESSING AT LABEL

The word following the instruction contains the address of the operand.

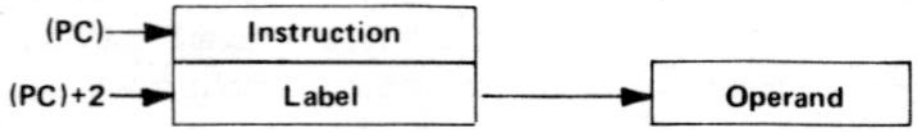

A.2.5 INDEXED ADDRESSING AT TABLE (R)

The word following the instruction contains the base address. Workspace register R contains the index value. The sum of the base address and the index value results in the effective address of the operand.

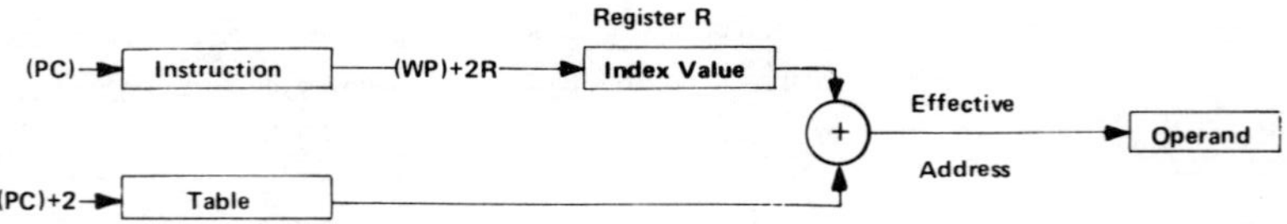

A.2.6 IMMEDIATE ADDRESSING

The word following the instruction contains the operand.

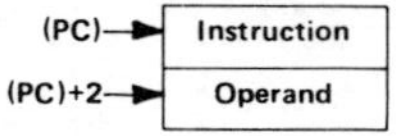

A.2.7 PROGRAM COUNTER RELATIVE ADDRESSING

The 8-bit signed displacement in the right byte (bits 8 through 15) of the instruction is multiplied by 2 and added to the updated contents of the program counter. The result is placed in the PC.

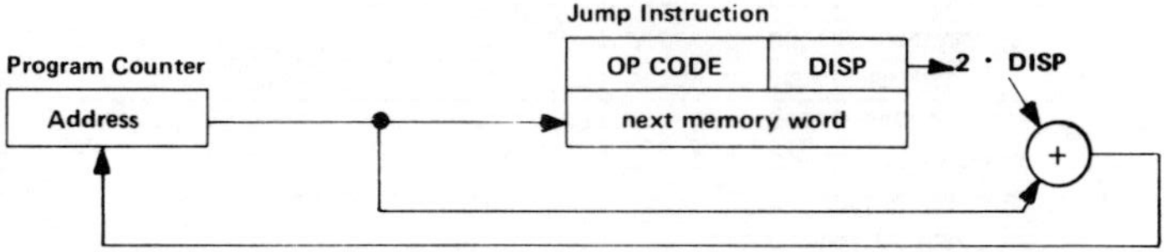

A.2.8 CRU RELATIVE ADDRESSING

The 8-bit signed displacement in the right byte of the instruction is added to the CRU base address (bits 3 through 14 of the workspace register 12). The result is the CRU address of the selected CRU bit.

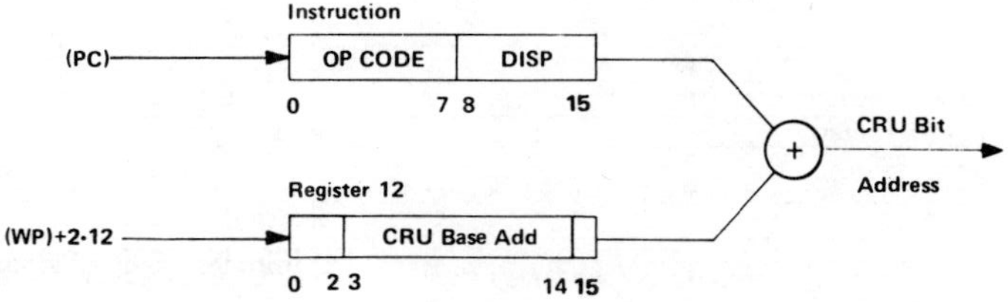

A.3 TERMS AND DEFINITIONS

The following terms are used in describing the instructions of the TMS 9900:

TERM	DEFINITION
B	Byte indicator (1=byte, 0 = word)
C	Bit count
D	Destination address register
DA	Destination address
IOP	Immediate operand
LSB(n)	Least significant (right most) bit of (n)
MSB(n)	Most significant (left most) bit of (n)
N	Don't care
PC	Program counter
Result	Result of operation performed by instruction
S	Source address register
SA	Source address
ST	Status register
STn	Bit n of status register
T_D	Destination address modifier
T_S	Source address modifier
W	Workspace register
WRn	Workspace register n
(n)	Contents of n
a → b	a is transferred to b
$\|n\|$	Absolute value of n
+	Arithmetic addition
–	Arithmetic subtraction
AND	Logical AND
OR	Logical OR
$\oplus$	Logical exclusive OR
$\bar{n}$	Logical complement of n

A.4 STATUS REGISTER

The status register contains the interrupt mask level and information pertaining to the instruction operation.

0	1	2	3	4	5	6	7	8	9	10	11	12	13	14	15
ST0	ST1	ST2	ST3	ST4	ST5	ST6	not used (=0)					ST12	ST13	ST14	ST15
L	A	=	C	O	P	X						Interrupt Mask			

A.5 DUAL OPERAND INSTRUCTIONS WITH MULTIPLE ADDRESSING MODES FOR SOURCE AND OPERAND

General format:

0	1	2	3	4	5	6	7	8	9	10	11	12	13	14	15
OP CODE			B	T_D		D				T_S		S			

If B = 1 the operands are bytes and the operand addresses are byte addresses. If B = 0 the operands are words and the operand addresses are word addresses.

The addressing mode for each operand is determined by the T field of that operand.

T_S OR T_D	S OR D	ADDRESSING MODE	NOTES
00	0, 1, . . . 15	Workspace register	1
01	0, 1, . . . 15	Workspace register indirect	
10	0	Symbolic	4
10	1, 2, . . . 15	Indexed	2,4
11	0, 1, . . . 15	Workspace register indirect auto-increment	3

NOTES:
1. When a workspace register is the operand of a byte instruction (bit 3 = 1), the left byte (bits 0 through 7) is the operand and the right byte (bits 8 through 15) is unchanged.
2. Workspace register 0 may not be used for indexing.
3. The workspace register is incremented by 1 for byte instructions (bit 3 = 1) and is incremented by 2 for word instructions (bit 3 = 0).
4. When T_S = T_D = 10, two words are required in addition to the instruction word. The first word is the source operand base address and the second word is the destination operand base address.

MNEMONIC	OP CODE 0	1	2	B 3	MEANING	RESULT COMPARED TO 0	STATUS BITS AFFECTED	DESCRIPTION
A	1	0	1	0	Add	Yes	0-4	(SA)+(DA) → (DA)
AB	1	0	1	1	Add bytes	Yes	0-5	(SA)+(DA) → (DA)
C	1	0	0	0	Compare	No	0-2	Compare (SA) to (DA) and set appropriate status bits
CB	1	0	0	1	Compare bytes	No	0-2,5	Compare (SA) to (DA) and set appropriate status bits
S	0	1	1	0	Subtract	Yes	0-4	(DA) – (SA) → (DA)
SB	0	1	1	1	Subtract bytes	Yes	0-5	(DA) – (SA) → (DA)
SOC	1	1	1	0	Set ones corresponding	Yes	0-2	(DA) OR (SA) → (DA)
SOCB	1	1	1	1	Set ones corresponding bytes	Yes	0-2,5	(DA) OR (SA) → (DA)
SZC	0	1	0	0	Set zeroes corresponding	Yes	0-2	(DA) AND $(\overline{SA})$ → (DA)
SZCB	0	1	0	1	Set zeroes corresponding bytes	Yes	0-2,5	(DA) AND $(\overline{SA})$ → (DA)
MOV	1	1	0	0	Move	Yes	0-2	(SA) → (DA)
MOVB	1	1	0	1	Move bytes	Yes	0-2,5	(SA) → (DA)

A.6 DUAL OPERAND INSTRUCTIONS WITH MULTIPLE ADDRESSING MODES FOR THE SOURCE OPERAND AND WORKSPACE REGISTER ADDRESSING FOR THE DESTINATION

General format:

0 1 2 3 4 5	6 7 8 9	10 11	12 13 14 15
OP CODE	D	T_S	S

The addressing mode for the source operand is determined by the T_S field.

T_S	S	ADDRESSING MODE	NOTES
00	0, 1, . . . 15	Workspace register	
01	0, 1, . . . 15	Workspace register indirect	
10	0	Symbolic	
10	1, 2, . . . 15	Indexed	1
11	0, 1, . . . 15	Workspace register indirect auto increment	2

NOTES: 1. Workspace register 0 may not be used for indexing.
2. The workspace register is incremented by 2.

MNEMONIC	OP CODE 0 1 2 3 4 5	MEANING	RESULT COMPARED TO 0	STATUS BITS AFFECTED	DESCRIPTION
COC	0 0 1 0 0 0	Compare ones corresponding	No	2	Test (D) to determine if 1's are in each bit position where 1's are in (SA). If so, set ST2.
CZC	0 0 1 0 0 1	Compare zeros corresponding	No	2	Test (D) to determine if 0's are in each bit position where 1's are in (SA). If so, set ST2.
XOR	0 0 1 0 1 0	Exclusive OR	Yes	0-2	$(D) \oplus (SA) \rightarrow (D)$
MPY	0 0 1 1 1 0	Multiply	No	·	Multiply unsigned (D) by unsigned (SA) and place unsigned 32-bit product in D (most significant) and D+1 (least significant). If WR15 is D, the next word in memory after WR15 will be used for the least significant half of the product.
DIV	0 0 1 1 1 1	Divide	No	4	If unsigned (SA) is less than or equal to unsigned (D), perform no operation and set ST4. Otherwise, divide unsigned (D) and (D+1) by unsigned (SA). Quotient → (D), remainder → (D+1). If D = 15, the next word in memory after WR 15 will be used for the remainder.

A.6 EXTENDED OPERATION (XOP) INSTRUCTION

General format:

0	1	2	3	4	5	6–9	10–11	12–15
0	0	1	0	1	1	D	T_S	S

The T_S and S fields provide multiple mode addressing capability for the source operand. When the XOP is executed, ST6 is set and the following transfers occur:

$(40_{16} + 4D) \rightarrow (WP)$

$(42_{16} + 4D) \rightarrow (PC)$

SA → (new WR11)
(old WP) → (new WR13)
(old PC) → (new WR14)
(old ST) → (new WR15)

The TMS 9900 does not test interrupt requests ($\overline{INTREQ}$) upon completion of the XOP instruction.

A.7 SINGLE OPERAND INSTRUCTIONS

General format:

0	1	2	3	4	5	6	7	8	9	10	11	12	13	14	15
OP CODE										T_S		S			

The T_S and S fields provide multiple mode addressing capability for the source operand.

MNEMONIC	OP CODE 0 1 2 3 4 5 6 7 8 9	MEANING	RESULT COMPARED TO 0	STATUS BITS AFFECTED	DESCRIPTION
B	0 0 0 0 0 1 0 0 0 1	Branch	No	–	SA → (PC)
BL	0 0 0 0 0 1 1 0 1 0	Branch and link	No	–	(PC) → (WR11); SA → (PC)
BLWP	0 0 0 0 0 1 0 0 0 0	Branch and load workspace pointer	No	–	(SA) → (WP); (SA+2) → (PC); (old WP) → (new WR13); (old PC) → (new WR14); (old ST) → (new WR15); the interrupt input ($\overline{INTREQ}$) is not tested upon completion of the BLWP instruction.
CLR	0 0 0 0 0 1 0 0 1 1	Clear operand	No	–	0 → (SA)
SETO	0 0 0 0 0 1 1 1 0 0	Set to ones	No	–	$FFFF_{16}$ → (SA)
INV	0 0 0 0 0 1 0 1 0 1	Invert	Yes	0-2	$\overline{(SA)}$ → (SA)
NEG	0 0 0 0 0 1 0 1 0 0	Negate	Yes	0-4	–(SA) → (SA)
ABS	0 0 0 0 0 1 1 1 0 1	Absolute value*	No	0-4	|(SA)| → (SA)
SWPB	0 0 0 0 0 1 1 0 1 1	Swap bytes	No	–	(SA), bits 0 thru 7 → (SA), bits

MNEMONIC	OP CODE 0 1 2 3 4 5 6 7 8 9	MEANING	RESULT COMPARED TO 0	STATUS BITS AFFECTED	DESCRIPTION
					8 thru 15; (SA), bits 8 thru 15 → (SA), bits 0 thru 7
INC	0 0 0 0 0 1 0 1 1 0	Increment	Yes	0-4	(SA) + 1 → (SA)
INCT	0 0 0 0 0 1 0 1 1 1	Increment by two	Yes	0-4	(SA) + 2 → (SA)
DEC	0 0 0 0 0 1 1 0 0 0	Decrement	Yes	0-4	(SA) − 1 → (SA)
DECT	0 0 0 0 0 1 1 0 0 1	Decrement by two	Yes	0-4	(SA) − 2 → (SA)
X†	0 0 0 0 0 1 0 0 1 0	Execute	No	...	Execute the instruction at SA.

*Operand is compared to zero for status bit.

†If additional memory words for the execute instruction are required to define the operands of the instruction located at SA, these words will be accessed from PC and the PC will be updated accordingly. The instruction acquisition signal (IAQ) will not be true when the TMS 9900 accesses the instruction at SA. Status bits are affected in the normal manner for the instruction executed.

Jump instructions cause the PC to be loaded with the value selected by PC relative addressing if the bits of ST are at specified values. Otherwise, no operation occurs and the next instruction is executed since PC points to the next instruction. The displacement field is a word count to be added to PC. Thus, the jump instruction has a range of −128 to 127 words from memory-word address following the jump instruction. No ST bits are affected by jump instruction.

MNEMONIC	OP CODE 0 1 2 3 4 5 6 7	MEANING	ST CONDITION TO LOAD PC
JEQ	0 0 0 1 0 0 1 1	Jump equal	ST2 = 1
JGT	0 0 0 1 0 1 0 1	Jump greater than	ST1 = 1
JH	0 0 0 1 1 0 1 1	Jump high	ST0 = 1 and ST2 = 0
JHE	0 0 0 1 0 1 0 0	Jump high or equal	ST0 = 1 or ST2 = 1
JL	0 0 0 1 1 0 1 0	Jump low	ST0 = 0 and ST2 = 0
JLE	0 0 0 1 0 0 1 0	Jump low or equal	ST0 = 0 or ST2 = 1
JLT	0 0 0 1 0 0 0 1	Jump less than	ST1 = 0 and ST2 = 0
JMP	0 0 0 1 0 0 0 0	Jump unconditional	unconditional
JNC	0 0 0 1 0 1 1 1	Jump no carry	ST3 = 0
JNE	0 0 0 1 0 1 1 0	Jump not equal	ST2 = 0
JNO	0 0 0 1 1 0 0 1	Jump no overflow	ST4 = 0
JOC	0 0 0 1 1 0 0 0	Jump on carry	ST3 = 1
JOP	0 0 0 1 1 1 0 0	Jump odd parity	ST5 = 1

A.8 CRU MULTIPLE-BIT INSTRUCTIONS

General format:

0	1	2	3	4	5	6	7	8	9	10	11	12	13	14	15
OP CODE						C				T_S		S			

The C field specifies the number of bits to be transferred. If C = 0, 16 bits will be transferred. The CRU base register (WR12, bits 3 through 14) defines the starting CRU bit address. The bits are transferred serially and the CRU address is incremented with each bit transfer, although the contents of WR12 is not affected. T_S and S provide multiple mode addressing capability for the source operand. If 8 or fewer bits are transferred (C = 1 through 8), the source address is a byte address. If 9 or more bits are transferred (C = 0, 9 through 15), the source address is a word address. If the source is addressed in the workspace register indirect auto increment mode, the workspace register is incremented by 1 if C = 1 through 8, and is incremented by 2 otherwise.

MNEMONIC	OP CODE 0 1 2 3 4 5	MEANING	RESULT COMPARED TO 0	STATUS BITS AFFECTED	DESCRIPTION
LDCR	0 0 1 1 0 0	Load communcation register	Yes	0-2,5†	Beginning with LSB of (SA), transfer the specified number of bits from (SA) to the CRU.
STCR	0 0 1 1 0 1	Store communcation register	Yes	0-2,5†	Beginning with LSB of (SA), transfer the specified number of bits from the CRU to (SA). Load unfilled bit positions with 0.

†ST5 is affected only if $1 \leqslant C \leqslant 8$.

A.9 CRU SINGLE-BIT INSTRUCTIONS

General format:

0	1	2	3	4	5	6	7	8	9	10	11	12	13	14	15
OP CODE								SIGNED DISPLACEMENT							

CRU relative addressing is used to address the selected CRU bit.

MNEMONIC	OP CODE 0 1 2 3 4 5 6 7	MEANING	STATUS BITS AFFECTED	DESCRIPTION
SBO	0 0 0 1 1 1 0 1	Set bit to one	–	Set the selected CRU output bit to 1.
SBZ	0 0 0 1 1 1 1 0	Set bit to zero	–	Set the selected CRU output bit to 0.
TB	0 0 0 1 1 1 1 1	Test bit	2	If the selected CRU input bit = 1, set ST2.

General format:

0 1 2 3 4 5 6 7	8 9 10 11 12 13 14 15
OP CODE	DISPLACEMENT

A.11 SHIFT INSTRUCTIONS

General format:

0 1 2 3 4 5 6 7	8 9 10 11	12 13 14 15
OP CODE	C	W

If C = 0, bits 12 through 15 of WR0 contain the shift count. If C = 0 and bits 12 through 15 of WR0 = 0, the shift count is 16.

MNEMONIC	OP CODE 0 1 2 3 4 5 6 7	MEANING	RESULT COMPARED TO 0	STATUS BITS AFFECTED	DESCRIPTION
SLA	0 0 0 0 1 0 1 0	Shift left arithmetic	Yes	0-4	Shift (W) left. Fill vacated bit positions with 0.
SRA	0 0 0 0 1 0 0 0	Shift right arithmetic	Yes	0-3	Shift (W) right. Fill vacated bit positions with original MSB of (W).
SRC	0 0 0 0 1 0 1 1	Shift right circular	Yes	0-3	Shift (W) right. Shift previous LSB into MSB.
SRL	0 0 0 0 1 0 0 1	Shift right logical	Yes	0-3	Shift (W) right. Fill vacated bit positions with 0's.

A.12 IMMEDIATE REGISTER INSTRUCTIONS

General format:

0	1	2	3	4	5	6	7	8	9	10	11	12	13	14	15
OP CODE											N	W			
IOP															

MNEMONIC	OP CODE 0 1 2 3 4 5 6 7 8 9 10	MEANING	RESULT COMPARED TO 0	STATUS BITS AFFECTED	DESCRIPTION
AI	0 0 0 0 0 0 1 0 0 0 1	Add immediate	Yes	0-4	(W) + IOP → (W)
ANDI	0 0 0 0 0 0 1 0 0 1 0	AND immediate	Yes	0-2	(W) AND IOP → (W)
CI	0 0 0 0 0 0 1 0 1 0 0	Compare immediate	Yes	0-2	Compare (W) to IOP and set appropriate status bits
LI	0 0 0 0 0 0 1 0 0 0 0	Load immediate	Yes	0-2	IOP → (W)
ORI	0 0 0 0 0 0 1 0 0 1 1	OR immediate	Yes	0-2	(W) OR IOP → (W)

A.13 INTERNAL REGISTER LOAD IMMEDIATE INSTRUCTIONS

General format:

0	1	2	3	4	5	6	7	8	9	10	11	12	13	14	15
OP CODE											N				
IOP															

MNEMONIC	OP CODE 0 1 2 3 4 5 6 7 8 9 10	MEANING	DESCRIPTION
LWPI	0 0 0 0 0 0 1 0 1 1 1	Load workspace pointer immediate	IOP → (WP), no ST bits affected
LIMI	0 0 0 0 0 0 1 1 0 0 0	Load interrupt mask	IOP, bits 12 thru 15 → ST12 thru ST15

A.14 INTERNAL REGISTER STORE INSTRUCTIONS

General format:

0	1	2	3	4	5	6	7	8	9	10	11	12	13	14	15
OP CODE											N	W			

No ST bits are affected.

MNEMONIC	OP CODE 0 1 2 3 4 5 6 7 8 9 10	MEANING	DESCRIPTION
STST	0 0 0 0 0 0 1 0 1 1 0	Store status register	(ST) → (W)
STWP	0 0 0 0 0 0 1 0 1 0 1	Store workspace pointer	(WP) → (W)

A.15 RETURN WORKSPACE POINTER (RTWP) INSTRUCTION

General format:

0	1	2	3	4	5	6	7	8	9	10	11	12	13	14	15
0	0	0	0	0	0	1	1	1	0	0	N				

The RTWP instruction causes the following transfers to occur:

(WR15) → (ST)
(WR14) → (PC)
(WR13) → (WP)

STATUS BITS

BIT	NAME	INSTRUCTION	CONDITION TO SET BIT TO 1
ST0	LOGICAL GREATER THAN	C,CB	If MSB(SA) = 1 and MSB(DA) = 0, or if MSB(SA) = MSB(DA) and MSB of [(DA)-(SA)] = 1
		CI	If MSB(W) = 1 and MSB of IOP = 0, or if MSB(W) = MSB of IOP and MSB of [IOP-(W)] = 1
		ABS	If (SA) ≠ 0
		All Others	If result ≠ 0
ST1	ARITHMETIC GREATER THAN	C,CB	If MSB(SA) = 0 and MSB(DA) = 1, or if MSB(SA) = MSB(DA) and MSB of [(DA)-(SA)] = 1
		CI	If MSB(W) = 0 and MSB of IOP = 1, or if MSB(W) = MSB of IOP and MSB of [IOP-(W)] = 1
		ABS	If MSB(SA) = 0 and (SA) ≠ 0
		All Others	If MSB of result = 0 and result ≠ 0

BIT	NAME	INSTRUCTION	CONDITION TO SET BIT TO 1
ST2	EQUAL	C, CB	If (SA) = (DA)
		C1	If (W) = IOP
		COC	If (SA) and $(\overline{DA})$ = 0
		CZC	If (SA) and (DA) = 0
		TB	If CRUIN = 1
		ABS	If (SA) = 0
		All others	If result = 0
ST3	CARRY	A, AB, ABS, AI, DEC, DECT, INC, INCT, NEG, S, SB	If CARRY OUT = 1
		SLA, SRA, SRC, SRL	If last bit shifted out = 1
ST4	OVERFLOW	A, AB	If MSB(SA) = MSB(DA) and MSB of result ≠ MSB(DA)
		AI	If MSB(W) = MSB of IOP and MSB of result ≠ MSB(W)
		S, SB	If MSB(SA) ≠ MSB(DA) and MSB of result ≠ MSB(DA)
		DEC, DECT	If MSB(SA) = 1 and MSB of result = 0
		INC, INCT	If MSB(SA) = 0 and MSB of result = 1
		SLA	If MSB changes during shift
		DIV	If MSB(SA) = 0 and MSB(DA) = 1, or if MSB(SA) = MSB(DA) and MSB of [(DA)-(SA)] = 0
		ABS, NEG	If (SA) = 8000_{16}
ST5	PARITY	CB, MOVB	If (SA) has odd number of 1's
		LDCR, STCR	If $1 \le C \le 8$ and (SA) has odd number of 1's
		AB, SB, SOCB, SZCB	If result has odd number of 1's
ST6	XOP	XOP	If XOP instruction is executed
ST12–ST15	INTERRUPT MASK	LIMI	If corresponding bit of IOP is 1
		RTWP	If corresponding bit of WR15 is 1

Index